KEN & JOULES TAYLOR

THE MAGIC OF
CRYSTALS
FOR HEALTH, HOME AND HAPPINESS

COLLINS & BROWN

INTRODUCTION

The beauty and power of crystals have long been recognized, from the obsidian, quartz and lapis lazuli adorning the ancient mask of Tutankhamen to the jaw-dropping designs of Swarovski that grace the catwalk, or even the sea salt flakes that are now an essential in every kitchen cupboard. From the bricks and mortar that make up our homes to the SIM cards in our mobile phones, crystals are an integral part of our lives.

Precious stones have been a lucrative trading commodity for well over five thousand years. Apart from useful stones, such as flint, which was mined and extensively trafficked in the Neolithic Age for dagger heads, even mere curiosities such as amber were transported for thousands of miles in the Bronze Age, along trade routes that reached from the Baltic Sea to the Mediterranean. The beauty of crystals has long been appreciated and their value remains high today.

But there is another facet to crystals. The search for new, cleaner sources of energy is a driving force in our modern world. Computer chips and smart watches contain quartz crystals, while silicon crystals are embedded in every tablet and smartphone. It is not surprising that some of us have become more and more interested in the power of crystals in our personal lives. After all, these stones are the products of natural forces such as ancient stars, the Sun, the movement of the Earth over thousands of years, and the heat of molten rock. We simply can't ignore their potency.

This book is a guide to your personal discovery of crystals. Divided into three main sections – Home, Health and Personal Power – with a smaller section exploring the relationship between crystals and the stars. There are loads of inspirational tips as well as project ideas for you to dip into, so you can unlock the power of crystals to enhance and rebalance every aspect of your life.

WHAT ARE CRYSTALS?

The word 'crystal' derives from the Greek for 'ice' and refers to an early belief that crystalline stones were simply water, which had frozen so solid that it was beyond thawing. As late as the 18th century, some scientists maintained that clear rock crystals were simply fossilized ice.

These days, we know that one atom of any single mineral is the exact replica of any other – atoms of gold, for example, are all identical – and this forms the basis of mineral classification.

A mineral composed solely of one type of atom is called an element, but most minerals are composed of a variety of different atoms, 'glued' together by electrical forces to produce molecules. A molecule of ice – the crystalline form of water – for example, is composed of atoms of hydrogen and oxygen arranged in beautifully ordered geometrical patterns.

We see the natural shape of water crystals in the snowflakes that drift from the sky in the freezing winter. The flakes grow, floating on the breeze, by collecting more and more molecules of water, which arrange themselves according to the characteristic hexagonal pattern of their atomic structure. Other minerals have a cube as their basic building block, or a pyramid; the wide variety of forms and shapes is one of the many things that makes crystallography such a fascinating subject.

Water is a mineral like any other. In polar landscapes, the hills, mountains, cliffs and even the ground itself consist of solid, crystalline water. Ordinary rocks are no different from this, except that the temperature at which they thaw is so high that we only see molten rock in the natural world in an active volcano.

Because of the high temperatures involved, many crystals are formed deep in the Earth or in volcanoes, where mineral-rich liquids slowly solidify in fractures in the Earth's crust. It is because different minerals freeze at different temperatures that we find such spectacular crystals as tourmalinated quartz, where tourmaline crystals seem to have penetrated rock crystal like magical arrows. Of course, it is the other way around: the tourmaline crystallized while the quartz was still molten and, when the quartz crystallized too, it simply enveloped the tourmaline.

Not all crystals rely on volcanic heat to form. Some minerals are soluble (salt, for example, dissolves readily in water) and when the mineral concentration in the liquid is high enough, the atoms start to stick together, forming crystals that are harvested by salt makers. Selenite, which can form distinctive desert roses, is one of the other minerals that crystallizes when sea water evaporates.

To further complicate the story of how crystals grow, it is worth noting that many minerals can crystallize in a variety of different shapes and forms. At first glance, the graphite 'lead' in a pencil bears no relation to a glittering diamond in a ring, but they are actually the same atomic element: carbon. The difference is that the diamond has been subjected to enormous pressure underground, so its atomic structure has been crushed into a more compact crystal lattice.

CRYSTALS, COLOUR AND LIGHT

The colour of many transparent stones is determined by minute traces of other minerals that suffuse the growing crystal. For example, ruby and sapphire are both made of corundum, which is colourless in its pure state. The reason they look so different is because ruby is coloured by chromium, whereas the other colours of corundum (which include yellow, green, pink and purple, as well as blue), are produced by the addition of iron and titanium in varying proportions.

Many minerals, however, are opaque, so light cannot shine into or through them (such as hematite, turquoise and basalt). Others are translucent, allowing only some light to shine through (moonstone, opal and tiger's eye belong in this

category). Some minerals produce such a range of crystal forms that specimens fit every category. Quartz, for example, is transparent in its pure form of rock crystal, translucent as carnelian, or opaque as jasper!

WHAT IS REFRACTION?

When light passes into a transparent mineral it is bent, a feature that can be demonstrated by plunging a pencil halfway into a glass of water: its shaft will appear to bend at the point where it enters the liquid. Some minerals bend light more than others; diamond, for instance, not only has a high degree of refraction but also a powerful ability to spread different wavelengths of light. Longer wavelengths (those towards the red end of the spectrum) pass through minerals with relatively little refraction, while shorter wavelengths (the blue-violet end of the spectrum) bend further. This effect, known as dispersion, accounts for the splitting of light into the spectrum by a prism, the appearance of a rainbow – where light is refracted through raindrops – and the sparkles from diamonds.

Many minerals (those whose crystal structures are not cubic) possess double refraction, whereby a beam of light entering them is split in two. Double refraction also causes dichroism, a property that causes a crystal to have one colour (or shade of colour) when looked at in one direction, and a different colour (or shade) when seen from another angle. These minerals absorb light differently according to what part of the crystal the light is travelling through. Optical calcite, kunzite and iolite all display strong dichroism.

Crystals hold many other fascinating optical effects. The iridescence of spectrolite and the glow of moonstone, for example, are attributed to layers of tiny inclusions that act like banks of mirrors, reflecting the refracted light. Minute flakes of the mineral mica also act like mirrors, and give stones such as aventurine their sparkle. Some minerals (such as certain specimens of rose quartz) have microscopic canals in their crystal structure, which are arranged at precise angles to one another, so that they channel light to produce distinctive rayed star patterns.

Light rays can also interfere with each other when reflected by an ultra-thin film, producing beautiful 'nebulous rainbows'. This light show – which has the same effect as oil on water – is perhaps best seen in opals, but fine cracks in rock crystal can put on an enchanting display, too, and on a much larger scale.

COLLECTING CRYSTALS

The price you pay for crystals depends on their rarity, size and form. A small natural amethyst, for example, will cost far less than a large hand-carved amber figurine. Most people build up crystal collections over time, buying a new stone when they can afford it and slowly discovering what is good value for money. Of course, you may be given gems as presents, or even enjoy prospecting for minerals (some can be collected quite easily; many can be picked up from beaches).

Although you are unlikely to come across fake gems, it is worth bearing in mind that, over the centuries, fraudsters have used trickery to transform base minerals into something more desirable. A favourite ruse is simply to dye the specimens: turquoise and chalcedony are particularly vulnerable to dyes. Then there are various forms of heat treatment that can be applied: citrine, for example, may be produced from either smoky quartz or amethyst. Sometimes, these alterations are only temporary and can cause the stones to degenerate drastically.

Though buying a talismanic crystal should be an occasion that is a bit more special than picking up groceries, it is also completely normal to buy a stone on impulse. If you spot a crystal that is truly irresistible, then it has already worked its magic. The fact that it can evoke a strong, spontaneous attraction means it has struck a chord deep within you.

The emotion a crystal conjures up – known as its 'resonance' – is one of the most important keys to using them as talismans. Treat the experience with respect: enjoy it, but don't abuse it. For example, if you find a stone to help overcome shyness, be wary of the temptation to shout it from the rooftops. If it's a stone to help you learn, don't go out celebrating instead of revising for an important exam, or you'll certainly learn something... the hard way.

You can tune into the resonance of a stone before you buy it. For example, if the crystal you desire is one with invigorating properties, you should do something that's energetic, or go somewhere that's buzzing with activity. If you are planning to buy a stone with calming properties, it's a good idea to visit peaceful places such as parks, libraries or galleries, or just take some time out and rest. Getting in the mood before you choose from the crystals on offer can help you prevent mistakes.

It is best to avoid buying stones with conflicting natures at the same time. If this is unavoidable, then at least carry them in different containers or pockets... and be aware that you may be prone to emotional turbulence on the journey home!

If you are able to see crystals before buying, often one specimen will stand out in a tray of similar stones, and you'll know at a glance that it's the right one for you. At other times, you may need to pass your palm over the selection, looking for a feeling of warmth emanating from the stone with the most harmonious resonance. Alternatively, you can handle each stone individually, feeling for a subtle tingling in your fingertips: the best stone for you will produce the strongest sensation. Some people mentally 'ask' the stone how it feels about going home with them. Occasionally, you might simply need to buy the one which is least easy to leave behind.

BRINGING CRYSTALS HOME

When you arrive home with your new stone, pause to savour the occasion before you unwrap it. Imagine you are about to welcome a new friend. You don't actually have to straighten the cushions and make cocktails, but you can certainly set the mood. Try playing some music suited to the nature of the stone. For example, if the crystal inspires sensitivity, put on something quiet and soothing; if it excites the passions, choose a rousing, upbeat tune.

If appropriate, you should open the package in the room where the stone is intended to have its greatest effect. Just as you are about to unveil it, consider for a moment the long journey that has brought the gem home to you. Think about its origin, perhaps geological eons ago in a country or sea that no longer exists, and imagine how and where it travelled up until the time that you first set eyes on it.

As soon as you open the package, engage either in the activity you hope it will promote or in a dramatic reconstruction – in your imagination if needs be – of that activity. Even the briefest attempt will empower the stone and help to make it more effective later. Crystals can quickly become charged with talismanic energy, and having them with you when you engage in the activity for which you bought them will strengthen their power.

Especially during the early stages of building a collection, it is well worth spending a few minutes examining every new addition in the company of each of your existing stones. Not only does this perform a sort of social introduction – and there is no need to feel embarrassed about entertaining this idea! – but it can also help you to discover or reacquaint yourself with any overlooked benefits, both physical and metaphysical, of the specimens you already possess.

CARING FOR YOUR CRYSTALS

Nothing lasts forever – not even diamonds, which gradually turn to graphite – so caring for your collection is the key to keeping crystals in good condition for as long as possible.

Some minerals, such as pyrites, begin to degrade as soon as they are taken out of the ground; they simply rust when exposed to air and the moisture it contains. Others, such as rose quartz, can start to lose colour if exposed to heat or bright light. Opals will lose their famous irridescence if handled too much (the grease from skin can penetrate and eventually dull this porous stone).

Other minerals, such as halite (rock salt) will start to dissolve if washed. Most, however, are very robust and – like the mountains from which they come – will easily outlast us.

It is rare for minerals to need more than a little light dusting from time to time and, in general, the less you fuss over them the longer they last. It is purely a matter of personal preference whether to keep them on show in an open bowl, or to treasure them carefully in a jewellery box.

AVOIDING MISHAPS

Some minerals are softer and more fragile than others. It is common sense to prevent them rubbing or banging against one another, as scratches and chips can occur in seconds, but the damage and regret can last a lifetime. It is always a good idea to check with the seller when you buy them if any stones require special care. Store your favourite or most precious crystals – especially those that are soft or fragile – in a jewellery box.

If you plan to use stones for healing (especially for crystal essence remedies, where they are steeped in water and the liquid is drunk, see pages 54–59), it is particularly important to get advice from the vendor about any problems in using the specimens you are thinking of buying.

One of the greatest joys of collecting crystals is sharing them with friends, so carry a number of your favourite specimens around with you, and leave others on display in your home.

HOME

Ancient or new-build, flat or mansion, any home can be transformed with crystals. By choosing stones carefully, you can enhance different aspects of any room, from using rock crystal clusters to brighten a dark hallway to warming up a living room with amber. This section will show you how crystals work with feng shui to promote harmony and inspire you with a host of decorative ideas. There are myriad ways to introduce crystal power into your home, and you don't have to be an expert to reap the benefits.

Over the millennia, mankind has called many types of dwelling home. Ancient civilizations raised substantial edifices of stone: the red city of Petra in Jordan, hewn from living rock; Machu Picchu, the lost Andean city of the Incas in Peru; and Angkor Wat, the city of 100 temples in Cambodia. Then there is Stonehenge, a prehistoric marvel of celestial architecture and, of course, the classical glories of Egypt, Greece and Rome. The sight of these stone structures can evoke in us unfamiliar and powerful sensations.

The materials from which our own homes are made can also affect us: most people can discern a difference in atmosphere between a cottage built of local stone and a tower block moulded from steel and reinforced concrete.

From the structure of our walls to the glass in our windows, from the metal nails and screws that hold everything together to the wires and plumbing that run like nerves and arteries under a skin of plaster and paint, a house is a construction of rock and metal. In fact, it is just like jewellery. The rocks differ, of course – jewellery is made from gemstones and precious metals instead of base brick and iron – but the parallels are worth considering, and even the prices can be comparable.

While 'houses' are refuges we build from the weather and the outside world, 'homes' are more intimate, affording us the luxury of moulding our personal environment to our individual tastes, a place where we can truly be ourselves. Yet most people don't have the option of owning the home of their dreams, or the resources to splash out on redecoration. Many live in rented houses and may not decorate as they please. One of the wonderful bonuses of using crystals is that you don't have to spend a fortune on expensive furnishings to dramatically improve your home.

KEY USES FOR CRYSTALS IN THE HOME

PROTECTION	Our homes provide security within their walls, from the weather, enemies or strangers. **Hematite** is unsurpassed in its qualities as a protective gem.
WARMTH	Warmth allows for comfort, relaxation and recuperation from the outside world. **Imperial topaz** represents the life-giving hearth.
NATURAL LIGHT	A dim home can have a profound effect upon us, not merely psychologically but physically. **Citrine** captures the essence of sparkling sunlight.
FRESH AIR	Air should flow freely through the home, reviving everything it touches. The clarity of **rock crystal** epitomizes the element of air.
CLEANLINESS	The antiseptic properties of **blue lace agate** are ideal in an area where cleanliness is a priority, such as the kitchen.
COLOUR	Being surrounded by favourite colours can help emotional and mental health. **Opal**, in its various forms, may help to inspire your colour scheme.
VIEWS	The direction in which your home faces has a bearing both on how it is decorated and what rooms are used for. Views may also be significant for the wellbeing of the inhabitants. **Moss agate** may inspire solutions.
SPACE	Whatever the size of your home or garden, making the most of space is a priority. A single **aqua aura** crystal, hung where it best catches the light, may prove particularly enlightening.
NEIGHBOURS	Often a prickly subject! **White moonstone** placed against an intervening wall will help to ease friction. In confrontational situations, holding a tumble-polished rock crystal may also prove useful.

THE ELEMENTS IN YOUR HOME

	FIRE	AIR	WATER	EARTH
ASSOCIATED WITH	Summer Noon South Red Hot and dry	Spring Dawn East Yellow/purple Hot and wet	Autumn Dusk West Blue Cold and wet	Winter Night North Green Cold and dry
ROOM	**Kitchen** The kitchen is the heart of the home, and is characterized by the heat of cooking.	**Living Room** A place for recreational and social activities, entertainment and study.	**Bathroom** Cleansing the body, calming the emotions and refreshing ourselves, here we also tend to wounds and soothe aches and pains.	**Bedroom** A place for rest, sleep and dreams.
SUGGESTIONS	Hang colourful transparent crystals in windows. Place red-veined ornamental stones, such as serpentine, with candles. Gem sculptures of animals, or fossil teeth and skulls, are also appropriate here.	Slices taken from large agate geodes make attractive wind chimes, or you could use crystal mobiles, transparent crystal spheres or clusters on windowsills. Gem sculptures of birds, or fossil insects in amber, work here.	The ideal room in which to place a bowl of tumble-polished gems, or an indoor waterfall filled with gems. Gem sculptures of fish, fossil fish and seashells also work.	Trycactus plants with tiny crystals as a gravel 'topsoil'. Pretty jewellery and storage boxes carved from opaque gems, gem sculptures of plants, or fossil plants, such as petrified wood.
ASSOCIATED GEMS	Carnelian Garnet Jasper Red amber Rose quartz Ruby	Amethyst Ametrine Fluorite Iron pyrites Kunzite Tanzanite	Aquamarine Azurite Blue lace agate Sapphire Sodalite Turquoise	Aventurine Emerald Jade Malachite Peridot Unakite

BASIC PRINCIPLES

The key to unlocking the full potential of your home is to work with it, not against it. With the help of crystals, you can warm up a cold room, shed light on a dark corner, enhance security and much more.

The appropriate stones can be placed in the affected part of your home, or carried as talismans. For example, if you wish to create more space, you could put an aqua aura in your pocket or purse. Every time you notice it, it will prompt you to reflect on your need for space; by being reminded of it in all sorts of places, at different times, a novel solution may spring to mind. Or placing the stone in the precise place where your need is greatest can spur you to look at your home in a different light. You might see a way to rearrange belongings or activities to give greater priority – and space – to the area.

If you need inspiration on redecorating a room, try taking a piece of opal with you when you go looking for paint or fabric swatches, or place it in a prominent position in the room you're considering, where it may help to inspire you.

To bring happiness and harmony into your home, it helps to explore its various components – somewhere to cook, relax, bathe and sleep – in the light of an ancient formula: the elements.

The four alchemical elements of fire, air, water and earth have been feted in the Western world for 2,500 years as containing everything necessary for life. When they are properly balanced in the correct proportions, they stimulate wellbeing and promote mental harmony. You can accomplish this balancing act by using crystals to enhance the appropriate elements of the rooms in your home.

The ancient formula also contains a fifth element – the spirit, or 'quintessence' – both nurtured by and bringing life to the four elements. In your home, this spirit is you, the soul who inhabits the material world composed of the four elements.

FENG SHUI

At the heart of the Chinese tradition of feng shui lies the notion of flowing. The words *feng shui* translate as 'wind and water', powerful elements that can be destructive in full force, or as gentle as a summer breeze. Feng shui is the art of working with the flow of another force, known as chi: the life energy that permeates the universe.

UNDERSTANDING CHI

Chi, the ancient sages proposed, is responsible for the wellbeing of every living thing. Like the wind, if you have too much you may be swept into disaster; like water, if you have too little you will grow weak and sick. But, in suitable proportions, chi is thought to bring both health and happiness.

Balancing yin and yang

In order for chi to flow, you need to make a channel for it: somewhere empty and somewhere full. These extremes – called yin and yang respectively – are perpetually merging as chi flows on.

By recognizing the qualities of yin and yang in everything around us, we can begin to understand the forces that govern the flow of chi. Then, if we see too much yin, we can balance it with yang, and vice versa. Using the yin-yang chart (see below), you can choose which type of crystal to use to correct any imbalance. For example, if a room feels empty, cold and dark – all yin attributes – then introduce some yang by adding sparkling, angular, white gems.

YIN		YANG	
Attributes	Gems	Attributes	Gems
Empty	Dull	Full	Sparkling
Cold	Rounded	Hot	Angular
Dark	Black	Bright	White
Relaxed	Amorphous	Energetic	Crystalline
Diffused	Composite	Focused	Pure
Passive	Opaque	Active	Transparent
Submissive	Soft	Dominant	Hard
Sleepy	Heavy	Alert	Light

USING THE CRYSTAL BA GUA

The crystal *ba gua* (see opposite) is a feng shui 'map' that can show you where to use crystals in your home. Simply overlay it on a ground plan of your home to see which stones will be most beneficial in each area. For example, you could place a piece of hematite on a north-east wall, perhaps by sticking small pieces on a mirror or picture frame, to boost education; or, to rekindle a relationship, try keeping malachite or bloodstone in the south-west area. Using harmonic stones in the correct positions means the circulating chi finds resonance and boosts the relevant aspect of life.

THE CRYSTAL *BA GUA*

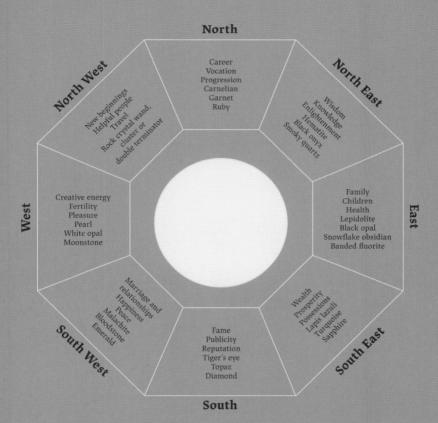

North

Career
Vocation
Progression
Carnelian
Garnet
Ruby

North West

New beginnings
Helpful people
Travel
Rock crystal wand,
cluster or
double terminator

North East

Wisdom
Knowledge
Enlightenment
Hematite
Black onyx
Smoky quartz

West

Creative energy
Fertility
Pleasure
Pearl
White opal
Moonstone

East

Family
Children
Health
Lepidolite
Black opal
Snowflake obsidian
Banded fluorite

South West

Marriage and
relationships
Happiness
Peace
Malachite
Bloodstone
Emerald

South East

Wealth
Prosperity
Possessions
Lapis lazuli
Turquoise
Sapphire

South

Fame
Publicity
Reputation
Tiger's eye
Topaz
Diamond

AREAS OF THE HOME

THE FRONT DOOR
The entrance to your home provides a welcome for you
and your family, friends and relatives, a pleasant view for
your neighbours and local community and a deterrent to
unwelcome strangers. There are many ways in which crystals
can affect everyone who crosses your threshold.

Guarding your home with sentinels
The sentinels are a pair of stones that should be positioned
on either side of the front path, near the entrance to your
property. Resembling the megalithic monuments of some
British Bronze Age stone rows, they represent the opposites in
nature: dark and light, winter and summer, woman and man,
the unknown and the known, yin and yang.

Depending on the size of your garden and budget, the sentinels
may be as small as fists or as tall as men, provided they are both
in proportion. The northerly, feminine sentinel should ideally
be low, rounded and broad. A dark-coloured stone is best but
a sedimentary rock, such as limestone, would also be fine.
Conversely, the masculine, southerly sentinel should be upright,
tall and pointed. A light-coloured stone is best, and an igneous
rock, such as granite, is preferable. (If your path falls directly
due north or south, then position the north sentinel to the west,
and the south sentinel to the east.)

The sentinels can be integrated into your garden in many
ways. You could allow moss to take hold, or small plants to
take root in crevices or pockets where a little soil will provide
sustenance, particularly on the feminine sentinel. If you wish
to grow flowers around them, you can plant a range of dark-
coloured, purple, deep blue or greenish blooms close to the dark
sentinel and, in contrast, light-coloured, red, orange, yellow or
white flowers close to the light sentinel. Such consideration will
enhance and boost their powers.

To further bolster their talismanic energy, place a small pebble (ideally a sphere) of a black crystal, such as obsidian, under the dark sentinel, and a similar orb of white stone (marble, perhaps) beneath the light sentinel.

As you walk between the sentinels, you pass through the point of balance at their centre and become the focus of life's harmonized energies. The stabilizing effect is two-fold, promoting mental equilibrium and a sense of proportion on the outward journey (where adventures, trials and temptations may await), and then again on your return, when the stresses of the day may be neutralized and left behind.

The sentinels are powerful guards that play an important role in protecting your property. In addition to the calming effect they will exercise on you, they may also exert a subliminal pressure on unwelcome visitors, perhaps presenting an obstacle to a cold caller or would-be intruder.

Creating a rainbow path
If you have a gravel path or driveway, you could perform a delightful ceremony of scattering a rainbow path. If you don't have a gravel path, you can gain the same effect by scattering stones among the hard core or concrete while laying a solid path or driveway. The path is a symbolic crystal bridge which links your home to the outside world, yet sets it apart in its own realm of peace and plenty.

To create the path, you need a selection of transparent or translucent stones, coloured if you like, though you don't need stones to represent all seven colours of the rainbow; instead, the emphasis is on beauty and intuition. You could choose a roughly equal number of blues, reds and greens of all shades and tints, or just use rock crystal. The smaller the stones, the better – even chippings are effective – because it is quantity not quality that counts. Once you have gathered a good amount of stones, leave them in a glass bowl on a sunny windowsill until you actually see a rainbow in the sky. At this point, dash out and carefully sprinkle them all along the path. Like sowing seeds of good fortune and joy, this can be done again and again.

The stones on a crystal path provide a way of approaching your home as a new experience: potentially wonderful, always unique and ultimately magical.

THE ENTRANCE, HALLWAY AND STAIRS
Entrance
The main entrance to your home is the door that is used most often, where you, your friends – and traditionally your luck – are welcomed in. A warm, south-facing entrance will benefit from a touch of the elements of air or water (see the yin yang chart on page 19) to balance any feelings of heat or oppressiveness, while a north-facing entrance may need the energizing element of fire to bring light and warmth.

Large specimens, such as a weighty crystal cluster or gem displays, create a memorable first impression in a hallway.

If you have ever had problems in rejecting cold callers, keep a dragon's eye near the front door. This powerful talismanic guardian will watch over the threshold and help keep undesirable guests at bay.

If the front door opens directly into a room, you may wish to form a divider to create a kind of small hallway. Rather like placing a rock in the middle of a flowing stream, this helps to prevent chi energy from running directly into the room and encourages it to circulate instead. Using a bookcase is perhaps the easiest means, providing shelves for crystals, candles and plants.

Feng shui principles advise that a front door should not be directly opposite a back door, because chi could flow in through the front and straight out at the back, bypassing the main part of your home entirely. Nor should the main door be directly opposite the stairs, since any chi accumulated in the upper storeys could flow down the stairs and straight out the front door. The easiest way to overcome these problems is to hang a gem mobile or wind chime (or both) from the ceiling just inside the door. A spiral pattern is most beneficial: it encourages chi's natural curving, flowing lines to spread through your home. Faceted 'crystal' glass is useful here, and will also scatter rainbows around the hall to create an appealing entrance to your home.

Stairways
Stairways are often dark places and can seem forbidding. They can also be focal point for accidents, so it is essential that they are kept clear of clutter, or distracting light and shadow play.

To make stairways more cheerful and to encourage chi to circulate upstairs, small rock crystal wands or delicate ornaments with faceted glass can be hung in windows, or you can place rock crystal clusters on a windowsill. If there are no windows, try positioning a mirror to illuminate a dark corner and hang a sparkling gem mobile in front of it to reflect and maximize the light.

Hallways
Hallways are the thoroughfares of your home and because you don't usually linger in them, they can seem rather neglected and impersonal.

However, as any true pilgrim will testify, the act of travelling is as important as the destination, so why not use the space offered by a bare wall for a display cabinet or shelving? This will provide the ideal opportunity to showcase a colourful variety of crystals and gems, particularly those that are better left untouched, such as fragile sulphur, or even cinnabar, which is beautiful but poisonous.

A dish piled with a selection of small, tumble-polished gems, placed where the light falls upon them, is ideal in the hallway.

THE LIVING ROOM
This is where friends are ushered on arrival and where family gather to enjoy leisure time. Often a busy, noisy area, where many different activities happen at once, the living room is traditionally connected to the element of air, and is often filled with electronic and digital equipment.

Where possible, the room should feel light and spacious, with furniture positioned around the sides to leave the central area free. This encourages the flow of chi and makes visitors feel more comfortable, as there's less risk of anyone creeping up behind them.

Generally, cool blues or greens are advisable for a hot south-facing room, and warm reds or yellows for a cooler north-facing one. There are exceptions, however.

A south-facing room overlooked by a hill or tall buildings can feel cold, regardless of how much sunlight enters, and the barrier can also obstruct the flow of chi. In this situation, hot colours and fiery stones such as topaz, yellow amber or tiger's eye can be an effective way of introducing warmth. The soft, soothing glow of lit candles can also work wonders.

If you have a hot, south-facing room, try using blue and green stones, such as green malachite and spectrolite, to help cool it down.

When choosing stones for this communal area, make sure you include rock crystal, the archetypal gem for air, and place the stone (ideally a sphere) where the sunlight can shine through it. Large specimens can be prohibitively expensive, but size is not an issue here. A small sphere with internal flaws will fill with iridescent rainbows and is actually more effective at promoting the free flow of communication than a large, clear stone.

Try hanging beaded curtains in a doorway or at windows. Clear, light purple, or golden-coloured gems are best, but beware if there are small children around that the curtains should be well out of their reach.

THE KITCHEN
The kitchen is often regarded as the heart of the home, so should always feel welcoming. When food is being cooked, it can get very hot, although as the kitchen is often situated at the cooler side of the house, the room itself can sometimes feel cold. To encourage a calm and comfortably warm atmosphere,

place a polished, rosy pink, opaque rhodochrosite or rose quartz on the windowsill. Pink minerals are associated with physical love and affection and epitomize the care that goes into feeding and nurturing a family.

To further balance the yang, place a bloodstone, with more green than red, beside the rosy stone. Green stones symbolize maternal love and remind us to take care in the kitchen, where the majority of domestic accidents occur. Or hang a piece of watermelon tourmaline in the window so light can shine through it. This translucent gem's pink and green hues represent both yin and yang in one unified whole, creating a feeling of family unity.

Avoid using crystal mobiles in the kitchen, as grease particles in the air quickly cloud transparent stones and cleaning them is tedious. To help distract you from mundane tasks, keep a strongly chatoyant mineral, such as tiger's eye, on a shelf or at eye level, where you can see it as you carry out your chores. A chatoyant gem has a band of light running underneath the surface that moves dependent on the light source.

The power of salt
One gem that almost everyone has somewhere in the kitchen is sea salt flakes, or rock salt. The grains of this show facets of its cubic crystalline structure.

Salt has been a tradable commodity since ancient times. Rock salt is generally mined from deposits left by evaporated primeval seas, which are still forming, for example at Great Salt Lake, Utah, in the United States. Places associated with salt mines were often named accordingly: Salzburg, in Austria, supplied ancient Rome. Sea salt flakes are manmade from heated seawater, but can nevertheless be beautiful.

People with surnames such as Salter probably had medieval ancestors who earned their living from the mining, transportation or sale of salt, which was once used in huge quantities to preserve food. Even the word 'salary' derives from the Latin word *sal* for salt, suggesting the high value placed upon this humble mineral.

Salt is symbolic of cleanliness, purification, human worth and, of course, the sea from which all life came. Keep it on view as a constant reminder of life itself, even if you choose not to display any other crystals in the kitchen.

THE DINING ROOM

These days the kitchen often includes both a cooking and dining area, which is not ideal in some respects, as the kitchen is symbolic of the element of fire while the dining area should be more earth-orientated. However, there are ways to achieve a harmonious ambience, such as to set the dining table cosily in a corner rather than in the middle of the room. This avoids obstructing the flow of chi and helps people sitting at the table (on the wallward sides anyway!) feel secure, which in turn aids digestion and promotes happy conversation.

Crockery and glassware can be chosen to suit the occasion and to create the right environment. Solid, earthy pottery and clayware, for example, is perfect for a serious heart-to-heart with a friend, as it reinforces the solidity of the relationship.

A more frivolous get-together would be better served by glass tumblers and bamboo or woven serving platters. A rock crystal mobile – or even a crystal chandelier if your dining room and budget can take it – can be hung above the dining table to aid the flow of chi and help keep the conversation buzzing.

A romantic dinner

A crystal landscape will create a feeling of intimacy and calm. Choose two candles of contrasting colours – warm rose red, and green or turquoise is a good combination – and glass or crystal candle-holders. Position them so they form a portal through which you can gaze at each other. Around the red candle's holder, place a selection of blue and green stones: chrysocolla, turquoise, aventurine. Around the other candle's holder, heap warm coloured stones: rose quartz, red amber, citrine.

Between the candles and slightly towards one of the place settings, position a rock crystal wand or a small jade obelisk or pyramid (a symbol of protection and the quest for knowledge).

On the other place setting, place either a rock crystal sphere, or a small jade sphere (symbolizing eternity and limitless potential). Rock crystal represents communication, while jade symbolizes love: either is appropriate here.

This arrangement carries several benefits. Firstly, the stones will help to earth an emotionally charged atmosphere, so you don't get carried away against your better judgement. They also act as reservoirs of bonhomie, smoothing over any potential sticky moments. But most of all they promote communication, both verbal and in terms of body language.

An informal lunch with friends
The emphasis for this sort of meal should be on easy conversation, laughter and fun.

Ideally, a bowl or chunky dish full of fairly large stones, placed among the food platters, forms both a talking point and a reminder that nourishment does not consist entirely of edibles: food for the spirit plays a significant part in life, too. Choose robust, non-porous stones so your friends can touch and handle them without fear. Try serpentine worry eggs, large pieces of rock crystal, and hematite spheres.

A business lunch
An attractive crystal centrepiece will encourage your lunch to run smoothly and successfully. A modern-day variation on the feng shui principle of the financially beneficial tank of goldfish is to put, in the centre of the table, a clear glass bowl of water, containing as many yellow and gold-coloured stones as you wish (uneven numbers are lucky). Tiger's eye is excellent for confidence and magnanimity, citrine for eloquence, rutilated quartz to help you stay up to speed. For extra luck, float three or five gold candles in the bowl, too.

THE BEDROOM
As we spend about one-third of our lives asleep, this room deserves considerable attention. A bedroom has four main purposes: the intimate expression of love and passion; sleep, where we recharge our batteries; dreaming, when our

subconscious minds order the day's events and summon the future; the room where we wake, ideally refreshed after a sound night's sleep.

According to feng shui principles, the bedroom should have as few internal corners as possible and the bed should be diagonally opposite the door. It may also be of benefit to align the bed on a north-south axis, so the bedhead is against a northerly wall. To neutralize a corner, place an artificial plant or a substantial stone on the floor there (provided you won't trip over it) or hang a crystal from the corner of the ceiling.

A screen, or room divider – or even a chest – between the bed and the door encourages the circulation of chi and creates a display point for plants and beneficial stones. Try hanging a crystal mobile just inside the door, or a crystal over the bed, to help you sleep.

Intimacy
To promote love and passion, display darker opaque stones in shades of purple, red and black, preferably with swirling patterns on their surfaces. Charoite, sardonyx, falcon's eye, lapis lazuli and tiger iron are all ideal.

Carved figures and statuettes are also perfect here. These can range from dragons carved from tiger's eye, jade or amethyst, to simple animal shapes inherent in the markings of the gem itself. Spheres and egg shapes representing fertility and femininity are also good, together with an upright crystal wand to balance them. Some people, even if they loathe snakes, may feel deliciously wicked in the presence of a jewelled cobra, while others might see a dragon's eye pig as a symbol of luxury and fun.

Sweet dreams
Certain stones may aid restful sleep. To help understand your dreams, keep a double-terminated rock crystal close by while you sleep. To promote a deep, healing sleep, try putting a tumble-polished piece of hematite under your pillow.

To help counter nightmares, place a large, smooth piece of moss agate or tektite by the bed where you can touch it. Its solid, reassuring feel will calm you if your sleep is broken.

If insomnia is a problem, try gazing into a small sphere or tumbled shape of green aventurine. Allow its soft, gentle hue, twinkling spangles of mica and smooth curves to lull you to sleep.

Finally, if you use an alarm to wake you, keep a chunk of clear yellow amber near the clock. As you switch off the alarm, pick up the stone. Holding something akin to solid sunlight in your hand before getting up can make all the difference to the quality of the day ahead!

THE BATHROOM

A place for calm, meditation, fun and pampering, the bathroom is associated with the ancient tradition of spas, which have been used for thousands of years by those in search of spiritual inspiration, relief from ailments and an escape from the world.

Yet bathrooms can be rather basic and functional, alternately hot and steamy or cold and clammy. To make yours more inviting, be bold and adventurous with its colour scheme, display plenty of fluffy, brightly coloured towels and put up shelves and display areas to show off crystals, plants and bottles of bath oil. Celestite adds an air of tranquillity, helping relaxation.

Transparent or translucent faceted, large crystals are best for the bathroom, as they won't be dulled by steam. Display bath salts, too, as these actually contain crystalline mineral salts. You could show off tiny gemstones in bottles, or hang rock crystal wands from the ceiling or shower-curtain rail. Try draping faceted crystals from wall sconces that hold candles. The lit candles will bring the element of fire into a room that inevitably contains so much water.

Keep a pumice stone handy (which is a healing stone in itself) both to smooth away hard skin and to remind you that not all beneficial stones are sparkling, crystalline display pieces.

Soak in the bath with your favourite healing stones, and keep some massage stones within easy reach for when you climb out of the tub. The best massage stones are large, smooth and rounded or smooth-ended wands, which you can use to gently rub and stroke the body.

Taking a bath can be a sensual experience or it can simply be fun: sprinkling a handful of bath salts into the water will liven up bathtime for children, who love to watch the way in which they fizz and dissolve, turning the water a different colour.

If you're feeling particularly stressed or tired, you could add a crystal essence remedy to the bathwater to soothe away the strains of the day, or refresh and revive the body (see pages 54–59).

THE GARDEN

Whether it is a small window box or rambling country acres, the garden is an ideal place for stones of all shapes and sizes. Try to channel chi energy into your garden by creating a water feature (preferably to the south), with a fountain or waterfall to keep chi moving. Surround it with large stones, perhaps containing mica flakes that sparkle in the light.

Arrange stones or shrubs along pathways to guide chi around the garden, soften corners with climbing plants, or better still, trees, and hang crystal mobiles from the branches. It may be possible to hang Aeolian chimes too, adding an element of soft music to the garden.

Earthing stones are also popular, acting as a point of contact with the earth deep beneath your feet. Like a lightning rod, it can conduct your thoughts to the ancient body of the earth, acting as a channel through which you may download all the conflicting energies picked up during day-to-day living.

This stone is arguably the most powerful stone you can use for cleansing, balancing and attuning yourself with the nature around you. It doesn't need to be large, provided it is positioned in a place of its own where it can radiate a sense of calm. It must be in direct contact with the soil and should ideally be made of the same sort of rock as the bedrock below ground in your own plot.

Whether you use your garden to cultivate fruit and vegtables or simply to relax and unwind, there are stones to suit the purpose. Here are some beneficial stones for a number of different requirements:

To grow healthy fruit and veg, try 'planting' a small stone at the same time as you plant seeds as a talisman to encourage them to grow. Malachite and aventurine, because of their association with fertility, are particularly good.

To boost the power of herbs, place a piece of hematite, smoky quartz or basalt at the base of each plant for strength and fruitfulness.

To promote rest and relaxation, choose large stones, such as ammonites and fossil-bearing rocks, and position them close to your favourite seats; hang sparkling mobiles of prehnite, tourmaline or amethyst from the branches of trees and bushes.

To enhance the view, chalcedony, smoky quartz, chrysoprase and dumorturite look beautiful when bathed in sunlight, because of their contrasts in colour and texture.

To create a peaceful atmosphere, rock crystals, amethyst spheres, labradolite and jade are all excellent stones for aiding tranquillity and meditation.

To make a focal point of a favourite container plant on the patio, you could incorporate crystals into or around the container.

THE OFFICE

Because work takes up a considerable part of our time, it is very important that our working environment is pleasing to the eye and conducive to mental wellbeing. If you work from home – as many of us do now, at least for part of the week – you may have to adapt part of a room as your office. But wherever you intend to work, there are a number of basic feng shui principles to follow.

Try to position your work station towards the east, to benefit from the yang chi engendered by the rising sun. If possible, you should have your back to a wall and use a high, solid bookcase or divider to separate the work space from the rest of the room. It may also be a good idea to create some kind of 'official' threshold to your work area, similar to the sentinels at the entrance to the house (see page 22). Indoors, you could use one tall and one short potted plant, or a couple of tables with crystal clusters prominently placed on top.

During the day, you can keep several favourite stones at hand, especially if your work involves staring at a computer screen for hours at a time. Contrasting shapes, colours and textures are ideal, for example a rock crystal wand, a large smooth piece of carnelian, or – a particular favourite – a smooth piece of polished labradorite.

To give your mind, eyes and fingers a break, devote a few minutes every hour to your crystals and admire the play of light, especially on those such as spectrolite, opal and moonstone and, of course, rock crystal with its characteristic 'rainbows'.

Of course, if you work in an office, many of these suggestions will apply to your desk or work space

ANXIETY AND CONFUSION

Inserted into the soil around the base of a plant on the desk or windowsill, a rock crystal wand can act as a mental lightning rod, earthing your stress and draining your mind of anxiety and confusion.

there, although you may have less choice about where those are situated. Crystals can personalize the space as they are portable, inconspicuous and very individual.

GOAL	COLOURS	STONES	ASSOCIATED WITH...
To boost self-confidence	Bright, sunny yellow stones	Topaz Citrine Tiger's eye	Courage Vitality
To aid communication when dealing with colleagues	White, pearly stones Rock crystals	Moonstone	Mental agility Quick-thinking
For growth, expansion and times of change	Green stones	Chrysoprase	Fertility Stability
For a competitive edge	Bright red stones	Ruby	Straightforwardness Strength in the face of adversity
In legal and financial matters	Blue stones	Lace agate	Business acumen
To help concentration in testing times	Black stones	Obsidian	Patience Fortitude
For inspiration	Purple stones	Fluorite	Dynamism Unconventionality
To foster compassion when sympathy and gentleness are needed	Soft turquoise-blue stones	Black opal	Sensitivity Perception
To boost critical abilities	Multi-coloured stones	Spectrolite	Self-analysis

CRYSTAL SOLUTIONS FOR THE HOME

GENERAL

PROBLEM	SOLUTION
Room(s) feel cramped and lacking in space.	Carry a single aqua aura crystal in your pocket or purse to inspire a novel solution. Or place the crystal in the affected room(s) to encourage you to see how to rearrange it to create more space.
You are worried about being burgled or are feeling insecure.	Display hematite, a protective gem, near the front door or other entrances.
Your home seems cold and damp.	Imperial topaz brings the essence of the life-giving hearth into your home, making it feel warmer and more comfortable.
The house is dark and does not get enough natural light.	Citrine captures the essence of sparkling sunlight, so will help brighten gloomy areas.
Rooms are stuffy and airless.	Place rock crystal in the affected rooms – it epitomizes the element of air and will help to banish staleness.
You are having trouble with neighbours.	White moonstone placed against an intervening wall helps to ease friction. In a confrontation, hold a tumble-polished rock crystal to calm things down.
After a stressful day, you tend to bring your problems home.	Create a rainbow path to your front door (see page 23), as this will help you forget the pressures of the outside world when you arrive home.
A warm, south-facing entrance or room feels hot and oppressive.	Introduce the elements of air and/or water by using stones such as iron pyrites, ametrine, amethyst, turquoise or azurite to cool it down.
A cold, north-facing entrance or room feels chilly and miserable.	Use stones such as carnelian, ruby, garnet, red amber, malachite, aventurine or jade, which represent the elements of fire or earth, to warm it up.
The back door of your home is directly opposite the front door, or the front door is opposite the stairs, going against feng shui principles.	Hang a gem mobile or wind chime from the ceiling just inside the front door.
The hallway is dark and forbidding.	Hang crystal wands in any windows, or illuminate a dark corner with a mirror and a sparkling gem mobile in front to reflect the light.
You are forced to move from a much-loved home into somewhere new.	Place a large rock crystal sphere where the sun can shine through it, or place sodalite or dumorturite at the front door to welcome new life experiences. Keep a bowl of tumble-polished rose quartz, milky quartz, amethyst and hematite beside your bed to help you sleep well and feel at home.

RELATIONSHIPS

PROBLEM	SOLUTION
You are hosting a party and are worried your guests may not get on.	Make a feng shui landscape (page 18) and use it as a centrepiece to foster harmony. Or place a small sphere of rock crystal on the table, preferably with rainbow-creating internal flaws, to promote the free flow of conversation.
Your bedroom is not a focus for intimacy.	Rekindle passions by displaying darker, opaque gems in shades of purple, red and black, preferably with swirling patterns. Charoite, sardonyx, falcon's eye, lapis lazuli and tiger iron are all ideal, as are carved figures and statuettes.
To keep the peace when in-laws (or other hostiles!) visit.	Wear or carry rose quartz to help foster warmth, peace and friendliness.
You find the atmosphere in the house depressing.	Use topaz, citrine and amber to bring some sunshine in, and hang wind chimes to add music. If you feel depressed about coming back home, try wearing amber jewellery and hang a rock crystal wand above the inside of the main door.

SLEEP DISORDERS

PROBLEM	SOLUTION
You suffer from nightmares.	Place a large, smooth piece of moss agate or tektite beside the bed, so you can reach out and feel assured by its weight and form.
You are a restless sleeper, or suffer from insomnia.	Place a piece of tumble-polished hematite under your pillow or try gazing into a small sphere or tumble-polished piece of aventurine, focusing on its gentle colour and soft curves to help you drift off to sleep.
You find it difficult to get out of bed in the mornings.	Keep a chunk of clear, yellow amber on your bedside table and pick up the stone as soon as your alarm clock goes off. This solid sunlight can give you a kick start, especially on a gloomy winter's day!

KITCHEN CHORES

PROBLEM	SOLUTION
When preparing food in the kitchen, you often cut or burn yourself.	Place a bloodstone, with more green than red, on the kitchen windowsill. Green gems symbolize maternal love and will remind you to take extra care.
You loathe mundane tasks such as washing up or preparing vegetables.	Keep a strongly chatoyant (banded, see page 27) gem, such as tiger's eye, on a shelf or at eye level to help distract you from your tedious chores.

HEALTH

CRYSTALS AND CHAKRAS

Before medicine discovered the viral and bacterial causes of many illnesses, the folk explanations for deadly epidemics and infections were often wildly fanciful. Demonic infestation or curses from angry spirits were common diagnoses and the only treatments for such dreadful plagues were often as dramatic as they were dubious... and sometimes horribly self-defeating. The belief that the Black Death of medieval Europe was caused by witchcraft led to the mass killings of 'witches' familiars' – aka cats – which were controlling the population of rats that spread the disease.

These days, people are becoming more interested in natural methods of staying healthy and traditional remedies, including crystal therapy, can be complementary to modern medicine. Crystals are thought to help cure ailments and, significantly, to maintain optimum health. Precisely how they work is hotly debated. A popular theory is that crystals actually vibrate at the same pitch as human beings, and can be used to relieve suffering because the resonance between patient and stone either combats the vibrations of illness or amplifies those of health.

A NOTE ON SAFETY
In this section, we explain a number of forms of crystal healing. However, it is generally accepted that these can take several sessions to be effective. If symptoms persist, or worry you, always consult your doctor.

HEALING WITH CHAKRAS

The chakras are part of an ancient and complex mystical system, devised in India and used by yogis as a path to enlightenment.

There are seven primary chakras located along an imaginary vertical line from the top of the head to the base of the spine. The practice of crystal healing with chakras is simply a matter of placing the appropriate stone on the chakra corresponding to the malady. It is believed that the natural affinity between stone and chakra retunes the chakra to a healthy vibration, thereby healing the part of the body affected.

CROWN OF THE HEAD	*(sahasrara)*	The gateway to spiritual illumination, profound joy and wellbeing.
BROW, OR THIRD EYE	*(ajna)*	Here, memory, dreams and psychic abilities may be strengthened and empowered.
THROAT	*(visuddha)*	The power of speech to communicate ideas and feelings is centred here.
HEART	*(anahata)*	Associated with love, this chakra may heal emotional relationships as well as the body.
SOLAR PLEXUS	*(manipura)*	Subjects as diverse as parent-child bonding and indigestion are dealt with here.
SACRAL	*(svadishthana)*	Apart from its physical aspect, this chakra relates to psychological sexual maturity.
BASE OR ROOT	*(muladhara)*	A firm foundation for living and the strength for self-development are focused here.

HOW CHAKRAS WORK

Each chakra represents a 'power point' in the human body and is associated with its own internal organs and systems: for example, the heart chakra is held to govern the entire circulatory system. Each is also connected with a colour and certain beneficial stones (see following pages).

The Sanskrit word 'chakra' conveys the meaning of a wheel, and yogis tend to think of chakras in this way, as wheels revolving. Yogis regard the chakras as the connections between the planes of purely mental energy and the physical energy of our bodies.

The chakras govern the flow of spiritual forces, or *prana*, which circulate along three channels (*nadis*) permeating the physical body. The central channel (*shushamna*) is associated with the spinal cord, while the other two (*ida* and *pingala*) are represented as serpents whose looping coils are entwined around the central column.

According to tradition, in a healthy body, *prana* should fill the chakras by rising up into them through the central channel of *shushamna*. Illness is caused when *prana* flows up into the chakras via the serpents, *ida* and *pingala*, therefore throwing the chakras out of balance.

Therapists also believe that the channels and chakras may become blocked. A blockage stops *prana* from filling the chakras properly, inhibiting natural behaviour or shutting down the immune system; it can also prevent energy from draining away, causing symptoms such as over-excitement, hyperactivity or obsessive behaviour.

DIAGNOSING THE PROBLEM

If you cannot pinpoint the source of an infirmity, or if an illness has a variety of causes, you may need help from an experienced practitioner. During a consultation, each chakra is checked in turn, often using a method called 'pendulum dowsing'. This is where the natural pendulum motion of a rock crystal, with a good pointed termination, determines in which area of the body a problem lies.

Because the wheels of the chakras are seen as revolving, the movement of the pendulum – either with or against the chakra's natural motion – provides a clear indication of its state of health. If the pendulum moves in tune with the chakra's natural motion, it is healthy; if it moves against the chakra's rhythm, it indicates that there is something wrong. When diagnosing chakras, the clearer the crystal you use, the more easily it transmits information.

Traditionally, a woman's crown (*sahasrara*) chakra revolves in an anti-clockwise direction (as viewed looking out from within your body), while that of a man rotates clockwise. The next chakra down (the brow, *ajna*) rotates in the opposite direction to the one above, and so on. So the lowest (base or root, or *muladhara*) chakra rotates in the same way as the top crown chakra.

As a general guide, you (or your patient if you are helping a friend) should be lying down comfortably, preferably flat on a bed or couch. Make sure the room is comfortably warm and not too bright, so the atmosphere feels soothing. You can even play relaxing music, light incense or burn fragrant oils to help you focus on the healing energy of the crystals during your therapy session, which can last 15–45 minutes.

Place the relevant stones (as many or as few as you like) either just on the chakra where the problem lies, or, preferably, on all the chakras leading up to it, putting the stones on the lowest chakra first and moving upwards. Concentrate on the crystals' energy, and try to visualize them working in harmony with the *prana* and each chakra, healing an area as the energies converge. This technique can also be used as a general tonic to strengthen and tone up the entire system, simply by placing a different beneficial stone on each of the seven chakras.

When you remove the stones at the end of the session, always remove the highest one first, leaving the lowest stone until last.

CROWN CHAKRA (*SAHASRARA*)

This chakra is most often imagined as a lotus flower with petals, no wider than your head, floating – as if your hair were the surface of a lake of crystal clear water – on the very topmost part of your scalp. The stem of this flower (which is generally visualized as having 1,000 petals) descends in a straight line through the body to the base of the spine, where it is firmly rooted.

While it is the aspiration of mystics to raise their consciousness from the root to the flower, to bask in the sun of spiritual illumination, we need only remember the picture of the serene lotus blossom to calm our minds. Twirling smooth pieces of stones, such as kunzite and charoite, while we imagine the sacred lotus growing, infuses them with a talismanic power that can help calm our nerves when needed.

Stimulating the *sahasrara* in this way can be used as a general tonic, and is recognized as having a powerful effect throughout the body, mind and spirit. The *sahasrara*'s influence can take a while to be noticed, as it attempts to harmonize and balance all the chakras beneath it simultaneously. However, these subtle benefits are cumulative and generally regarded as the key to maintaining good health.

The *sahasrara* is also regarded as the gateway through which spiritual energy enters the physical body. If it becomes

Chakra healing for insomnia
Other conditions that are regarded as particularly susceptible to crystal healing using this chakra include stress-related insomnia. As a healing solution, place the chosen crystal beside your bed, or under the pillow. As you settle down to sleep, picture the thousand-petalled lotus flower that symbolizes this chakra, bathed in warm sunshine and floating on the gentle swell of a crystal clear lake.

STONES	COLOUR
Kunzite, charoite, rock crystal	Violet

blocked, problems arise because the spiritual forces that normally flow into and through us – and our lives – can no longer invigorate and cleanse us. Such problems often seem to manifest in symptoms, such as lethargy and apathy, alienation and loneliness.

BROW OR 'THIRD EYE' CHAKRA (*AJNA*)

Generally regarded as being situated between the eyebrows in the centre of the forehead and just inside the skull, this chakra has also been identified with the pineal gland in the brain that distinguishes between day and night and secretes melatonin.

The *ajna* is at the heart of our ability to imagine, dream and see visions. It is an 'eye' in the mind that sees a world full of hidden meaning and exciting mystery. It is also the centre of psychic and spiritual intuition. This chakra is often stimulated in an attempt to develop psychic abilities, such as telepathy.

Healing this chakra can help to ease the suffering caused by persistent or severe headaches and migraines, recurring nightmares, depression and anxiety. The eyes, ears, and nose are also said to benefit from treatments administered here.

Conditions such as earache, sinusitis and blurred vision are all traditionally treated by stimulating the *ajna*. Even a nasty head cold, with the misery of a blocked nose and runny eyes, can be eased by a gentle massage between the brows with tumble-polished stones, such as amethyst or lepidolite. Stimulating the *ajna* can also help to improve memory and is particularly recommended for students studying for exams. Results cannot be expected overnight, but significant effects may begin to be noticeable after two or three sessions.

STONES	COLOUR
Amethyst, lepidolite, purple fluorite	Purple (indigo)

THROAT CHAKRA (*VISUDDHA*)

This chakra is connected both with the power of speech and with the sense of self-worth that gives us the power to express ourselves. Many people who feel shy and unable to share their feelings with others benefit from stimulating the *visuddha*.

Any blockage in the channel which allows us to voice our opinions and give vent to our emotions can cause deep anxiety and unhappiness, cutting us off from the world in which we live. Because this blockage prevents fluent self-expression, it also prevents other people from getting to know the sufferer, contributing to deeper social isolation. Working with this chakra can help alleviate these problems by reinforcing self-confidence and opening up the mind's natural channel of communication: speech.

The *visuddha* may also be stimulated in order to foster eloquence and the ability to make yourself perfectly clear. Anyone having to make a speech, give a presentation, or even engage in one of the performing arts that require a strong voice, can benefit from working on the *visuddha*. Some people actually use this chakra to help tone down a tendency to be arrogant, self-righteous and overbearing.

Thyroid problems, tonsillitis, laryngitis, a hoarse voice and sore throat are among the conditions treated using this chakra (a crystal essence gargle made with rock crystal may also soothe them, see page 59).

Stress often causes uncomfortable tension in the back of the neck and shoulders, and this is another malady that can be relieved by focusing on the *visuddha*. This chakra can spread its healing energies right down through the shoulders, flowing along the limbs and into the hands. Like the voice, the hands are particularly important for self-expression.

STONES	COLOUR
Sapphire, turquoise, sodalite	Blue

HEART CHAKRA (*ANAHATA*)

The effect of stimulating this chakra can be felt throughout the body, just as the blood pumping through our veins reaches every extremity. With a little practice, you can feel your pulse throughout your body and also sense the flow of the heart chakra's healing energy.

In physical healing, the *anahata* is widely used to counteract problems with circulation. For example, low blood pressure can be treated with a light green stone (such as chrysoprase); high blood pressure can be treated with a dark green crystal (try dioptase) – but, as always, consult your doctor too.

Through its association with the thymus gland, the *anahata* is also stimulated in an effort to boost the immune system and fight infection. Healthy people can use this chakra to fortify the heart, if physical activity is planned, and there is a need to feel energetic. Similarly, if a period of increased stress is foreseen, then working with the *anahata* may help strengthen emotional balance and prevent loss of temper or feelings of bewilderment.

Mood swings are particularly responsive to treatment here. It is thought that pre-menstrual tension can benefit from the stimulation of the *anahata*, especially if the sufferer begins daily sessions several days before their period is due.

Of course, the heart is also associated with love and applying stones here can help us to recognize (and share) our feelings for colleagues, friends, family and partners. The *anahata* may also help people come to terms with past mistakes and even find a way to love themselves: a fount of self-healing.

STONES	COLOUR
Emerald, jade, aventurine, malachite	Green

NAVEL CHAKRA (*MANIPURA*)

The name *manipura* translates as 'city of jewels', which gives an impression of the glories that a clairvoyant might see when contemplating the navel chakra.

The *manipura* is particularly important: while of little practical use post-birth, the navel is still a vital part of our being. It is the emblem of the maternal bond, the love that a mother has for her child. That powerful energy can be tapped through this chakra and it helps us face up to our responsibilities towards other people, as well as to the animals that share our world.

Anyone wishing to have a more active social life, especially with a view to attracting a partner, can use this chakra to boost their personal magnetism.

Emotional insecurity and panic attacks can have a devastating effect, but both respond well to treatment here. Obsessions (especially a compulsion to keep control) and phobias are also treatable here.

A wide range of genetic disorders and inherited illnesses are also treated at this chakra point and, although healers tend to stimulate it to ease discomfort rather than effect any particular cure, the therapy can still be very beneficial indeed.

This chakra is responsible for digestion and healers stimulate it to treat conditions such as ulcers, irritable bowel syndrome, morning sickness and trapped wind. Diabetes, diseases of the liver, such as hepatitis, and also gall bladder problems, such as gall stones all come under the influence of the navel chakra.

Place the stone in the navel to promote maternal bonding energy, or beside the navel to treat the digestive system.

STONES	COLOUR
Yellow topaz, yellow amber, iron pyrites, rutilated quartz	Yellow

PELVIC CHAKRA (*SVADISHTHANA*)

Identified with the primary sexual organs, this chakra is associated both with the physical process of conception and with the powerful psychological urges of human sexual maturity. Many people experience difficulty coping with the pressure that our sex drive exerts on our behaviour. Whether it is inhibited or overactive, the *svadishthana* is employed as a counterbalance, and working with this chakra can help to bring these urges into a healthy and naturally harmonious state.

Although the mood swings that characterize adolescence are best treated in the *anahata* (see page 50), stones appropriate to the *svadishthana* – tiger's eye in particular – can be beneficial for developing teenagers (even if only carried in a trouser pocket). The same holds true for women entering menopause.

Adult women who experience acute period pains are also offered treatment at this chakra point, a series of sessions being held in the days prior to their period. An expectant mother can use this chakra to strengthen herself against premature birth and labour pains.

**Chakra healing
for pre-menstrual tension**
Carry one of the stones listed below with you. When you have the opportunity, gently rub it over your lower abdomen, starting just below the navel. Move in a large circle towards your left, then let the circle become a spiral towards the middle. Focus on the warmth flowing from the stone, bringing deep comfort and relaxation.

STONES	**COLOUR**
Orange jasper, tiger's eye, sunstone	Orange

ROOT CHAKRA (*MULADHARA*)

The name *muladhara* is composed of two Sanskrit words meaning 'root' and 'support'. Think back to the image of the glorious white lotus flower that blossoms in the crown chakra (see page 46); here, in the *muladhara*, are the strong, hungry roots that delve deeply into the thick, fertile silt at the bottom of the lake and hold the whole plant, with its long stem, securely fixed in position.

The base chakra represents a firm foundation for our entire being: its primal energy is what keeps us going when we are alone and things get tough. This chakra is situated at the base of the spine and is associated with the anus.

Crystals should be placed so that they are actually resting on the ground between the legs, their position corresponding to the base of the spine. The colon also comes under its sphere of influence and medical conditions affecting this part of the body are suitable for therapy using the *muladhura*.

Problems with the legs and feet also benefit from the healing energy radiating from this chakra and make it especially popular with healers, who regularly use it to ease the suffering caused by conditions such as sciatica, rheumatism, arthritis, varicose veins and bunions. Sporting injuries that affect the legs and feet (such as torn tendons and sprained ankles) are also particularly susceptible to therapeutic energies released by this chakra.

Furthermore, these benefits are often extended to assist with faster healing and strengthening of broken bones in the legs and feet. Because of its effect on the lower limbs, athletes and sports players can also use the base chakra to help build up and tone this part of their body so that they obtain the maximum benefit from training and can compete more successfully.

STONES	COLOUR
Ruby, dragon's eye, carnelian, garnet	Red

CRYSTAL ESSENCE REMEDIES

This is a modern version of an ancient tradition in which special stones are immersed in pure water to extract their healing essence, in much the same way as herbs are steeped to make a herbal tea.

The theory behind crystal essence remedies lies in the belief that a crystals' curative properties percolate into the water and are transferred to the liquid, which absorbs and stores these subtle forces. The liquid can be drunk to combat a specific ailment or simply taken as a preventative and general tonic. The illnesses that respond best to this therapy are those caused by a mental, emotional or spiritual blockage or imbalance, so it is particularly good for stress-related conditions.

Crystal essence remedies will not cause any obvious side effects and are comparable to flower essence remedies.

Crystal essences, particularly rock crystal, can also be used to mist the home and house plants as well as being poured into bath water to allow you to bathe in the healing energy of the stones. You could even make up an essence as a gift for a relative or friend who is unwell or under some kind of stress.

Before preparing your crystal essence remedy, refer to the list of common ailments (see pages 58–59) to find out which stone you need.

HOW TO MAKE YOUR OWN ESSENCES
First, choose a stone or stones that are hard and smooth. This is important because the stones and the glass container should be hygienically clean, so flaky or powdery stones, or those that have cavities which could harbour micro-organisms, are not suitable. The stones must also be pure: not embedded in or alongside any other (potentially dangerous) mineral in the same specimen. And remember, where more than one form of a particular mineral exists, it is only the most solid or crystalline form that should be used.

Once selected, some practitioners like to purify, balance and charge their stones before using them to make an elixir. You can do this by placing them in the midst of a rock crystal cluster for up to two hours. This process can also be repeated after the stones have been taken out of the liquid, cleaned and dried. To prepare your crystal essence:

1. Place the appropriate stone in a glass tumbler, jar or bottle.

2. Fill the vessel with enough water (preferably pure mineral water) to completely cover the stone.

3. Cover the container to prevent contamination. (Before use, the liquid should be kept as free as possible from contamination by micro-organisms.)

4. Put the container in a safe place where it can bask in as much direct sunlight as possible, or in moonlight if preparing an essence that is meant to calm, relax or boost receptivity. You can leave it to steep for anything from one minute to 12 hours. (If you prepare a moonlight essence before going to bed, you can take a few drops in the morning.) The longer the immersion, the stronger the essence will be.

5. Strain the liquid from the stone.

USING CRYSTAL ESSENCE REMEDIES

Before and after you drink the essence, a few minutes' rest is recommended as, although the elixir helps healing to happen, it is your own life force that actually brings it about.

If the stone has only been soaking for a minute or two, you may drink all the liquid. If it has been submerged for up to one hour, take a few sips only; if submerged for up to six hours, take one small sip only. If the stone has been immersed for over six hours, take a few drops of the liquid only.

You can also mix the elixir with alcohol to form a tincture, which will extend its shelf life. In this case, you should use distilled water and, after draining the liquid from the stone, add an equal quantity of brandy. Take only a few drops of the tincture in one dose.

You can repeat the dose several times a day but, of course, if you still feel run down, medical advice should be sought. It is usually advisable to use an essence on the same day it is made, unless you bottle it and store it in the refrigerator, where it will last for several days. Tradition dictates that it should never be frozen into ice, the crystal form of water, because this destroys its curative properties. If more treatments are needed, prepare fresh essence – just clean and dry the stone before re-using it.

Safety guidelines

Many minerals react with water on a chemical level. (Salt, for example, dissolves.) Because some minerals, such as galena, are poisonous if taken internally, some stones mentioned in this book are *not* appropriate for crystal essence remedies. So if in doubt, follow the recommended suggestions (see pages 58–59) or seek professional advice.

STONES TO RELIEVE COMMON AILMENTS AND CONDITIONS

Whether your pain is physical, mental, emotional or spiritual, crystal remedies can help. Although you should always see your doctor if you have any health problems, especially if an illness is prolonged or suddenly severe, crystals can help to relieve minor ailments and promote general wellbeing. Now that you know how to prepare a crystal essence remedy, you can refer to the comprehensive list of common problems (see following pages) to choose your crystal cures. In addition to making the essences, to treat physical pain you can also try rubbing the crystal against the part of your body that is causing distress.

CRYSTAL SOLUTIONS FOR HEALTH

EMOTIONAL DIFFICULTIES

PROBLEM	ASSOCIATED STONE
Difficulty in overcoming sexual inhibitions	Garnet
Insomnia, stress	Rhodochrosite
Lack of confidence	Aventurine
Overactivity	Star sapphire
Nervous tension	Apatite
Fear of the unknown	Tourmalinated quartz
Sexual anxieties	Smoky quartz
Insecurity	Nephrite jade
Depression	Rutilated quartz
Lacking understanding	Blue lace agate
Poor judgement	Sodalite
Poor memory	Amber
Fear of making mistakes	Azurite
Nerves, anxiety	Epidote, diamond
Inability to let go of attachments	Tanzanite
Repressed anger and fear	Rose quartz
Lack of inspiration or receptivity	Moonstone
Negative self-image	Citrine
Difficulty expressing love or emotion	Dioptase
Difficulty in raising consciousness	Bloodstone

PHYSICAL AILMENTS

PROBLEM	ASSOCIATED STONE
Headache, neuralgia, sunburn, high temperature, minor burns and scalds, muscular aches, sprains	Red carnelian, red jasper
Tense neck and shoulders, sore throat, laryngitis, halitosis	Malachite, aventurine
Warts, dry and chapped skin, colds, flu	Tumble-polished rock crystal
Indigestion, swollen breasts during menstruation	Moonstone, milky quartz
Backache, poor circulation	Citrine, rutilated quartz
Menstrual cramps, irritable bowel syndrome	Rock crystal egg
Sciatica, lower back pain, numbness from sitting for too long at a desk, incontinence	Chrysoprase, peridot
Premature ejaculation, vaginal dryness, low libido	Snowflake obsidian, moss agate
Rheumatism, lowered resistance to disease, overeating	Sodalite, turquoise
Toothache, acne, bone fractures, joint pain	Hematite, obsidian
Cramp, broken veins, hyperventilation, phobias, panic attacks	Amethyst, lepidolite
Corns, verrucae, chilblains, water retention, dependency on caffeine, alcohol or tobacco	Chrysocolla, aquamarine
Sluggishness, lethargy, a need to invigorate the entire body	Rock crystal
A need to promote all healing	Watermelon tourmaline
Inability to relax	Malachite

SPIRITUAL ISSUES

PROBLEM	ASSOCIATED STONE
Inability to transcend dogma	Charoite
Unable to feel universal love	Iolite
Lack of spiritual insight	Labradorite
Obstacles to developing psychic abilities	Sapphire
Inability to recognize spiritual messages	Lapis lazuli

PERSONAL
POWER

We all have dreams, hopes and desires, and crystals can help us achieve them. Whether you want to unlock your inner potential, find love, or enjoy material success, a crystal talisman can help. You can even use pendulum dowsing (see page 79) to get in touch with your subconscious mind. Whatever your aspirations, this chapter shows how crystals can help you find happiness and success.

USING CRYSTALS AS TALISMANS

We can all think of things we'd like to change about ourselves and the world in which we live. If you were given a magic wand, how long would it be before you used it to make a few improvements in health, wealth, or love?

Anything can be talismanic, provided it means something to you. Talismans are like stepping stones, helping us fulfil our dreams: some are broad and secure; others demand a sure eye and nimble feet.

Crystals and other stones have been used for centuries to represent hopes and wishes. By choosing the stones that best reflect your own desires and wearing them, or carrying them around, you can tap into this traditional power.

A bold necklace of blood-red rubies makes a loud statement that the wearer is full of confidence and looking for excitement. Delicate earrings of blue celestite, on the other hand, speak to the wearer's gentle and contemplative character. We all have instinctive emotional responses in the face of such clear signals. Learning to use jewellery to send a message is an art in itself. Crystals and other minerals are capable of more subtle effects, too, and talismanic magicians have for millennia used the different elements of the natural world to affect their lives.

Self-empowerment using crystals works at the same level as our human capacity for seeing something that move us to tears, or raises our hopes. Although the stones trigger our responses, we ourselves are the source of the magic.

HOW TO CHOOSE YOUR TALISMAN

Think long and hard about what it is that you really want. You can even write a wish list, so you can review it when you need to. Then put your list to one side. When you come back to it later, try to prioritize the areas in your life that you are most likely to be able to change (set aside, but don't discard, the least promising). Once you have decided on your goal, you will probably find that a sequence of events will lead you to it. At this stage, any number of different talismans can be used to help you towards each separate target, while one particular crystal – representing your ultimate goal – can be used constantly.

Here, we suggest a suitable stone for different areas of your life that you might want to focus on.

GOAL	STONE
New beginnings: moving house, starting a new job, or having a baby.	Topaz
To direct energy towards a work goal; try carrying this when requesting a pay rise!	Rock crystal wand
To calm a tempestuous romance and encourage consideration in your partner.	Peridot
To promote leadership. Try wearing it for success in competition.	Ruby
To assist concentration. Keep a piece near your desk.	Black flint
To encourage responsiveness to the ideas of others, and overcome obstructive single-mindedness.	Spinel, sardonyx
To promote stability, combat insecurity and attract treasures (especially antiques).	Amber
To encourage sensuality and enliven a slow metabolism. Keep in the bedroom and don't handle too often.	Desert rose
To help dispel resistance to change and promote mental adaptability. Keep in the workplace.	Rock quartz cluster
To help overcome stubbornness and self-sabotage. Most beneficial when worn as earrings.	Garnet
To help overcome self-indulgent tendencies. Keep in front of the mirror!	Azurite nodules

GOAL	STONE
To create self-discipline at work, especially when you seek work-life balance.	Galena (this is toxic, so handle with care)
To promote constructive thinking and mental resourcefulness.	Charoite
To enhance artistic inspiration and appreciation; useful in art and music tests and interviews.	Chrysocolla
For common sense. Used as a worry stone, it can help you see the funny side.	Unakite
For skill in dealing with colleagues and make speaking to authority figures easier.	Citrine
For situations where clear communication is necessary.	Rock crystal double terminator
To encourage affection for others. Useful on a first date, or when socializing with people you don't know well.	Moldavite
To develop keen powers of observation.	Fire opal
To promote ease of expression, especially if you find conventional education difficult.	Moldavite
To assist in ordering chaotic thinking, creating a logical approach to problem solving.	Stibnite
To promote spontaneity and flashes of insight.	Ametrine
To help overcome impractical tendencies.	Aqua aura
To develop self-analysis or help break bad habits.	Onyx
For protection or to promote caution. Useful to keep on your desk, especially in a new job.	Aragonite
To help alleviate digestive or eating disorders, or promote a calm atmosphere. Useful for busy mothers.	Moonstone
For overall protection against the tribulations of life. It may help you endure them with patience and humour.	Silver
As a meditation stone, to develop good memory and quick understanding, especially of children.	Tumble-polished rock crystal
To promote maternal feelings and the ability to cherish others.	Amazonite
To help alleviate stress-related illness, combat frustration (especially in the home) and a tendency to moodiness.	Rose quartz
To promote excellent interpersonal relations. You can wear this at work.	Blue moonstone
The ultimate protective stone; used for deflecting negative influences and encouraging tolerance. It may also help control panic attacks.	Specular hematite
To encourage responsiveness to emotional stimuli, and promote self-confidence.	Smithsonite (copper bearing)

GOAL	STONE
To improve tenacity and willpower, especially in personal relationships.	Turritella
To lessen your dependence on the approval and opinions of others.	Ammonite
To encourage deep understanding of your inner resources, and develop the willpower for success.	Tiger's eye
Embodies beauty, confidence and creativity and can be worn to promote these qualities.	Diamond
To help combat arrogance and encourage a willingness to learn.	Rainbow aura
To create faithfulness and physical energy; ideal to wear or keep (perhaps as a carved animal) in the bedroom.	Malachite
To encourage nobility of ideals, help banish fear of matters beyond your control and help deal with guilt.	Sodalite
To develop a sense of realism and pragmatism.	Smoky quartz
To encourage selfless love and altruism. Useful in the home, especially if there are children about.	Watermelon tourmaline
To promote justifiable pride in your achievements. Useful for those who have been ground down, so feel they have nothing to offer.	Leopardskin jasper
When rational thinking and a logical approach to problem solving are required.	Petrified or opalized wood
To help speed recovery if you're feeling under par.	Milky quartz
To focus your mind when contemplating the future, or as a worry stone if you feel insecure (especially at work).	Rock crystal egg
To bring out the gentle side of intimate relationships.	Epidote
To help overcome shyness or nervousness.	Rhodochrosite
To aid personal integrity. Can help you stand firm when under pressure to act against your better judgement.	Lace agate
To combat overly critical or fault-finding tendencies, in yourself or others.	Mauve opaline
When precision or attention to detail are required. Promotes perfectionism and critical judgement.	Larimar
To encourage analytical skills, or calm nerves when you feel control slipping, especially if others cause problems.	Brecciated jasper
To encourage honesty. Use when you suspect companions are being less than truthful, or to give yourself the nerve to be honest.	Selenite
To combat indecisiveness when faced with difficult choices, or even if you can't decide where to go for dinner!	Faceted rock crystal
To promote enjoyment of the simple, natural things in life, especially if you feel life is becoming too complicated.	Chrysoprase

GOAL	STONE
When you want to be fair in your dealings with others and want them to be fair in return.	Pink tourmaline
If you are too easily swayed by others, try using this to contemplate the worth of your own beliefs.	Blue agate
To encourage impartiality and diplomacy.	Black onyx
To help ease a situation in which you have to compromise to keep the peace, whether you want to or not.	Sugilite
To help combat a tendency to be overly sensitive; criticism is often designed to be helpful, not malicious.	Malachite, azurite
To help overcome low self-esteem and foster self-confidence.	Snowflake obsidian
For helping self-control and self-reliance. Beneficial for those who feel at the mercy of others.	Golden beryl
To help bring your inner beauty to the surface, where it may be admired.	White opal
To enhance your perceptiveness and ability to keep secrets. Useful for those who tend to gossip.	Rainbow quartz
To promote passion and a love of the dramatic. Ideal for the bedroom!	Bloodstone
To encourage self-reliance and resourcefulness.	Red aventurine
To help overcome manipulative tendencies, both your own and those of others.	Falcon's eye
To guard against loss of emotional control, especially in intimate or hostile circumstances.	Black calcite
To promote inner peace, strength and an appreciation of the need to conserve resources, both your own and those of the planet.	Serpentine
To stay young at heart and bursting with vitality.	Rutilated quartz
To promote independence and an inquiring mind. Excellent for those leaving home to study or train.	Clear calcite
To encourage willingness to try new experiences. Useful for those about to go on an adventurous trip.	Prehnite
Embodying benevolence, optimism and wisdom, this may be worn to engender and enhance these qualities.	Sapphire
Symbolizing spirituality and strong moral codes, you can wear this to strengthen against temptation.	Turquoise
To restore your faith in the human race and also help curb an extravagant streak.	Lapis lazuli
To promote dependability and economy. Can be useful to carry when shopping, to avoid overspending.	Yellow jasper

GOAL	STONE
To help temper materialistic and mercenary qualities. Can be handy to keep at work if you find the atmosphere unfriendly.	White chalcedony
When mental clarity is required or to curb pedantry. May prove beneficial when taking exams.	Rock crystal geode
To promote constancy in love and engender protective tendencies. An ideal gift for a loved one, or for new parents.	Jade
To enhance sexual stamina; keep by the bed to liven up your romance.	Red jasper
To help curb selfishness and promote ambition for others, especially children.	Natural azurite
For endurance and determination and to help you overcome obstacles in your life.	Jet
To help enhance professionalism in your chosen career.	Eilat stone
To promote prosperity and growth, this general luck-bringer may be used in both business and private life.	Moss agate
To remind you of the possibility of change and potential for human development in us all.	Brown zircon
To help shed light on problems and dilemmas, making them easier to solve.	Optical calcite
To create objectivity and clear-mindedness. Anyone involved in education can benefit from keeping this with them.	Rock quartz sphere
For those wishing to break out of a rut, to help promote freedom of thought, speech and lifestyle.	Aventurine
To encourage humanitarianism. Useful if you wish to counter bigotry or prejudice.	Rhodonite
For those who tend to rely on stimulants (coffee, tobacco, alcohol) to keep going when they should rest, this may enable natural relaxation.	Aquamarine
To encourage the ability to absorb information. Try keeping a worry egg or smooth piece at your desk where it can be handled.	Orthoceras
To enhance receptivity and generate a sense of humour.	Rock crystal phantom
To promote devotion and selfless love. This is an ideal stone to use as a focus of meditation during a retreat, as it can enable you to commune with your inner self.	Dioptase
To inspire novelty and playfulness in sexual matters. Keep some by the bed.	Dragon's eye
To help enhance intuition and imagination, or to bring out artistic talent.	Amethyst

HOW TALISMANS CAN HELP

Talismans can be regarded as 'keys', capable of unlocking a future which had seemed closed to you. But if they are such powerful tools, why isn't everyone using them? The answer is that everyone is. Many of us have trinkets or clothing that we regard as lucky and – from that favourite shirt to the bike you ride – everything has its own talismanic power and purpose.

You can't wear a lucky shirt every day, but crystal talismans can accompany you anywhere. Carry them in a pocket or purse, or wear them as jewellery. A talisman's power radiates like an aura, simultaneously protecting you from misfortune and failure and stimulating the optimum conditions to speed you on to your goal.

Simply twirling a stone between your fingers can invoke its power immediately, whenever it is needed. Even when you are unconsciously toying with the stone you can reinforce the wish and quickly draw out its power to help.

TOP 10

LOVE LIFE
CRYSTALS

Q
Do you want to strengthen a relationship
or get to know someone better?
A
Emerald will help build and develop a rapport.

Q
Are you having to choose between potential
(or current) lovers?
A
Moldavite can help you make the right decision.

Q
Are you so infatuated by someone that you can't think straight?
A
Amazonite will help you get your feet on the ground
and think clearly.

Q
Has your relationship become staid and boring,
or is it going nowhere?
A
Choose malachite to give it a new dimension.

Q
Are you worried about moving in with a partner,
or settling down?
A
Epidote will help you understand what living together
could mean; emotionally, financially and practically.

Q

Do you feel the balance of power in your relationship
is uneven?

A

Chrysoprase can promote harmony, help partners relax
and enjoy each other for who they are.

Q

Are you unconvinced by the power of love?

A

Bloodstone will show you that love can move mountains
when both partners are dedicated to one goal.

Q

Are outside pressures taking their toll on your relationship?

A

Prehnite or wavellite will help overcome worries that
seem beyond you.

Q

Are you unfulfilled or stuck in an unhappy partnership?

A

Aventurine can help you break away from unloving,
destructive relationships.

Q

Are you investing so much into your relationship that you
don't have a life outside it?

A

Dioptase can help you to find a passion outside the relationship.

TOP 10

LEARNING
CRYSTALS

Q

Are you nervous or worried about the first day of a course?

A

Carry black flint on the first day to help break the ice
with colleagues.

Q

Do you think you might find it difficult to settle
into the college or class?

A

On the second day, take basalt with you to help you
develop a routine.

Q

Finding it difficult to take in so many new facts and figures?

A

Once the course is under way, black onyx can help you
assimilate and weigh up large quantities of data.

Q

Have you been invited to attend a social event
or party during the course?

A

Black tektite could allow you to project non-scholarly
aspects of your personality.

Q

How can you put all those new ideas and information
to best use?

A

Pick fire opal to inspire and motivate you.

Q

Is your course accountancy-based?

A

Lace agate may help you keep long-term goals for this field
clearly in mind.

Q

Is your course an artistic one, such as creative writing?

A

Amethyst is your ideal talisman.

Q

Do you tend to put off doing course homework,
or fail to do as much as you should?

A

Kunzite will help promote self-discipline and
a responsible attitude.

Q

Are you feeling nervous about leaving home to study
or for training?

A

Take clear calcite with you to promote independence
and an inquiring mind.

Q

Do you find it difficult to concentrate?

A

Use a rock crystal wand to help focus your mental energies
into your work.

PURIFYING YOUR TALISMANS

Talismans quickly become charged with memories. They have
the potential to become as precious to you as a favourite
souvenir, like the pebble that takes you back to a wonderful
beach holiday. However, just as stones are believed to be
storehouses of healing energy or talismanic power, they can
also soak up impressions from their environment, some of
which may be undesirable. It is a good idea to rid the stones
of these unwanted elements by cleansing or purifying them.

You may use earth, fire, air or water to purify your stones,
provided the stone can withstand the treatment. If the stone is
fragile or of uncertain provenance, you may also decontaminate
it quickly by resting it for a while in a rock crystal cluster.

Whichever means you use to purify the stone, you may
wish to recite a few appropriate words. For instance, at the
commencement of the purification, try: 'Welcome [name of
mineral], in the hope of strength, truth and beauty, I offer you
purification by the element of [earth/water/air/fire].' After the
allotted time, you may add: 'Purified by [earth/water/air/fire]
in the trust of strength, truth and beauty, I treasure you [name
of mineral].'

FIRE

Allow the stone to bask in sunshine for one hour.
Or place it within a circle of three white candles
and allow it to sit in their flickering light for one
hour. (Never leave burning candles unattended.)

AIR

Lightly toss the crystal through
plumes of incense smoke.
Repeat this a total
of nine times.

EARTH

Wrap the stone well in non-
synthetic cloth. Bury it in
the ground, no deeper than
the distance from wrist to
fingertip. Leave it for three
nights and retrieve it on the
third day.

WATER

Immerse the stone in fresh still water, changing
the water three times a day for a full three days.

GIVING TALISMANS MORE POWER

To bring out a stone's innate qualities and imbue your talisman with additional power, you can make it the focus of a simple ritual, surrounding it with colours, metals and scents that naturally radiate the energy you want to harness. It is actually very straightforward.

To choose a ritual that best suits you, choose from the chart on page 78. A stone is suggested for each scenario, along with the day when you should perform your ritual, the metal and the scent you should bring. Arm yourself with an item of the appropriate colour, or wear clothes in that colour, find the right place for your ritual and you're ready.

Hold the stone and concentrate on your desired purpose. Feel the strength of your will flowing into the stone: close your eyes and feel an answering warmth flow back from the stone and into you. Imagine the stone becoming a friend and a situation where the talisman is going to assist you. When you find your concentration slipping, it's time to stop. Gently breathe on your stone to complete the cycle.

You can make your ritual as elaborate or simple as you like, incorporating elements other than those suggested (for example, you can use incense, candles and even music that summons up the essence of your desired result). You are creating your talisman, so make the ritual as intensely personal as you wish.

THREE KEY RITUALS

You can use your talisman for a more involved personal ritual that will attune the stone to you and boost its power to help you achieve your goal. Bringing in elements of the easy rituals already suggested, this takes a little longer and requires some concentrated effort, but the benefits are invariably worthwhile.

Do not start working with your new stones until you are happy that they are not carrying any distractions for you. If, for example, you keep thinking of its previous owner whenever you look at a stone, or you imagine some inexplicable event or sensation, you may like to cleanse the stone again (see page 72). When you feel comfortable with the crystals, you're ready to connect to the energy they represent.

Allow 30–90 minutes for the ritual, choosing a comfortable place where you will not be disturbed and where you can use a surface, such as a clear coffee table, dressing table, or even a space on the floor.

Are you under pressure at work or home and suffering from stress as a result? Do you always seem to be struggling to make ends meet, or feel that you deserve a pay rise? Or perhaps you have been unlucky in love and would like to reverse this trend? If your answer to any of the above questions is 'yes', then one of these three key rituals could be the answer to your problems.

THE STRESS BUSTER
Iron pyrites is the perfect talisman for dealing with overall stress and its unpleasant effects.

Gather together some **yellow and grey-green** candles. You could also incorporate these colours into decorations, perhaps using a grey-green tablecloth or backdrop and yellow flowering house plants, for example.

The ritual should be performed on a **Sunday** and any gold item may be set beside the pyrites. If an incense or perfume with a **fresh scent** can be used, so much the better. Before the ritual, you might like to snack on something **sweet**. If you have time, you could take the iron pyrites to a **public garden or art gallery** where it can soak up the atmosphere, since you will easily be able to conjure up the image of the place in your mind, and even use it as a refuge when stress is at its worst. Or you could place a keepsake – such as a painting, photograph or postcard of a garden or gallery – beside the stone during the rite.

Alternatives

If your stress is work-related, choose **fire opal** as your talisman to help you make good decisions about how to prioritize your workload. Alternatively, try using a **rock crystal wand**, as this stone might spark a new idea as to how to reorganize your working practices and to communicate your plan to your boss, or someone with the authority to take action.

THE WEALTH BRINGER

To attract wealth, luck and opportunity, **sodalite** is the ideal talisman.

Schedule your ritual for a **Thursday** and choose candles and a colour scheme in shades of **blue and gold**. Gather together any items made of brass and scents or perfumes with a particularly **warm, intoxicating odour**. Coins and bank notes, being representative of wealth, may also be liberally scattered around.

Prior to the ritual, take your talisman to a place that symbolizes wealth, such as **a bank, a jewellers, or an expensive hotel**. It isn't necessary to go inside if you don't want to, but try to touch the wall of the building. Before performing the ritual, treat your taste buds to some **rich food**.

Alternatives

If you need money urgently, you could use **star sapphire** or **falcon's eye**. If you are hoping to soon reap the financial benefits from a long-term project, then **sapphire** is your best bet.

THE PATH TO LOVE

The perfect stone for attracting a new lover is **peridot**. The best day for your rite is a **Friday**, and as **green and scarlet** are the appropriate colours, the room could be decorated with candles, tablecloths, flowering plants and so on in these vibrant and beautiful hues.

The **scent of citrus** would strike the right note and any personal souvenirs of **hilltops or sporting competitions** would also help to attract and project the right energies.

Any items made of **copper** will add strength to the rite, which can also be enhanced with personal touches to indicate the kind of lover you are hoping to attract. Red roses, for example, would suggest that you're out to attract a romantic, while a golf ball or tennis racquet would imply that you're keen to catch a sporty partner!

Alternatives
If you want to attract the attention of someone you already know, then **emerald** would be more suitable.

HOW LONG BEFORE YOU SEE RESULTS?
As a rule, talismans exert their power continually and at a constant level. They work in a subtle but cumulative way, so although it may take time to see any effect, your talisman will have been working behind the scenes, clearing obstacles and setting up the potential for your goal to be realized.

However, you can also draw off talismanic power from the stones in bursts. When you specifically need their powers, all you have to do is to concentrate on them and reconnect with their special nature.

If, at any time, a stone starts to be intrusive and becomes a distraction, leave it alone for a while. If you are still having problems with it, then the stone should be thoroughly cleansed and re-energized.

TEN SIMPLE RITUALS

GOAL	STONE	DAY	METAL	SCENT	COLOUR	WHERE
To improve career prospects	Ruby	Tuesday	Iron, such as an iron nail	Citrus	Scarlet	A place associated with competition, such as a playing field
To attract love and romance	Emerald	Friday	Copper, such as a copper bangle	Pine	Deep green	A spot where there are plenty of roses, such as a rose arbour
To bring more opportunities into your life	Rock crystal double terminator	Wednesday	Tin, such as a wire	Herbal	Palest blue	Near a stream or river
For personal balance and to relieve stress	Chrysoprase	Friday	Copper	Fresh	Grey-green	Anywhere that feels restful and harmonious
To help you change and take control of your life	Serpentine	Sunday	Steel, such as cutlery	Musk	Red, black	An out-of-the-way, solitary place
To bring luck in legal and financial matters	Sapphire/ sodalite	Thursday	Brass, such as a door knob	Woody	Royal blue	Under the canopy of a mature tree, such as an oak
For calm and endurance when taking tests	Jet	Saturday	Lead, such as a lead crystal glass	Smoky	Black	Somewhere quiet where you can concentrate easily
To help you find like-minded friends and get on with colleagues	Kunzite/ amethyst	Monday	Titanium, such as in a mobile phone	Sharp	Bright purple	Somewhere that makes you feel invigorated
For health and wellbeing	Rock crystal egg	Wednesday	Tin	Floral	Pale yellow	In a garden blooming with flowers
To assist you in spiritual quests	Black opal/ spectrolite	Any, but Thursday may be slightly more favourable	Platinum, such as a ring	Exotic	Turquoise	Ideally by the sea, or somewhere that makes you think of the ocean

PENDULUM DOWSING

Pendulums offer an inexpensive and absorbing way to reveal and experiment with your psychic abilities. Forked sticks have been used to find underground water for many centuries, and although pendulums may be a recent extension of the ancient tradition of dowsing, they have gained a dedicated and enthusiastic following.

Pendulums can be used for a wide range of purposes, from treasure hunting, prospecting for precious metals, locating missing persons and lost pets, fortune telling, determining the sex of unborn children and fun party games. Part of the appeal of this form of dowsing is the ease with which anybody can investigate and use the power of the pendulum.

Project: making and holding your pendulum
A dedicated dowser might invest in a specially ground and flawless rock crystal pendulum, drilled at one end and attached to a fine silver chain. However, almost any smallish rock crystal wand will reveal your aptitude. The wand should be 2–3cm (¾–1in) long and hung by a thread so that the natural facets of the crystal point hang down, pointing to whatever is being dowsed. The thread should be around 30cm (12in) long and may be fixed to the crystal with strong glue. Natural fibres, such as cotton, hemp or wool (but not silk) in white or purple are best, or even silver. If your wand has a rough or knobbly base around which the thread or chain can be secured without glue, so much the better.

If you plan to use your pendulum outdoors, where strong wind can be a serious handicap, then the pendulum can be heavier and larger (6–8cm [2¼–3in] long and hung from a cord or chain about 50cm [20in] long). In this instance, basal features to which the cord or chain can be tied are particularly helpful.

When holding a pendulum, most people instinctively grip the thread between the forefinger and thumb of their dominant hand. However, when dowsing for long periods of time or with a heavy pendulum this grip can become tiring, which can interfere with the sensitivity of the instrument. A popular alternative is to hold the thread in the palm of your non-dominant hand using your thumb and all of your fingers except the forefinger.

The forefinger is extended (as if pointing to something) and then slightly crooked. The thread is then simply hooked over the furthermost section of the finger; you should avoid getting it caught in the crease of the joint itself. This arrangement provides maximum sensitivity with a high degree of comfort.

If the pendulum is a little heavy, it may be dangled over the middle section of the forefinger or, if it is particularly large, you can drape the thread across the strongest bone of the finger, the section closest to the knuckle.

If you are dowsing an object, such as a map, which can be placed on a table, by all means sit down and make yourself comfortable. Many dowsers actually rest their elbow on the table to avoid being distracted by tired arm muscles.

Using your pendulum

The pendulum communicates in a very simple way: it either stays still; swings gently to and fro in an arc, which may widen into an oval, and then become a circle; or swing in a full circle right from the start, which may narrow into an oval, then become an arc. The oval or circle can have a clockwise or anti-clockwise direction.

If you are just beginning to experiment with your abilities, it is worth spending some time just holding the thread and letting the pendulum twirl and gyrate with random motion. This is called the starting position and gives you time to settle down and feel comfortable with what you are doing. Just watch it for now. Don't try to get it to answer any questions but simply get used to the way it feels to have it dancing freely around.

In most forms of divination there is an accepted way of doing things. Pendulum dowsing is different. Most authorities agree that you must conduct your own experiments to interpret the pendulum's movements: there are no hard and fast rules to follow.

This may sound daunting, but it really is very simple. All you need to do is ask the crystal to respond to a few straightforward questions and, by observing the shape of its answers, you can quickly decipher its language.

It is worth noting that, if you have difficulty in getting the pendulum to move at all, you can deliberately set it moving in an arc – this will be your starting position – and the answers to your questions will then be determined by the direction (clockwise or anti-clockwise) in which the pendulum starts to move.

Getting started

The best way to begin is to ask a question to which you would expect to receive a 'yes' response. Hold the pendulum (in the starting position) so that it dangles a couple of centimetres above the palm of your empty hand. Ask a question where you know yes will be the answer.

Now place a pen on the table and ask the question, 'Is this an apple?' If it seems to make the same motion as before, when it answered 'yes', then clearly something is wrong and more practise is required! But if it responds in a completely new way then this can be interpreted as the 'no' response.

It is worth noting here that, although a few people do seem to have an immediate affinity with dowsing, everybody is advised to check and double-check the responses (using as wide a variety of subjects as possible) before putting their pendulum to use in an important situation.

Using your pendulum in everyday life

Because the pendulum can amplify minute movements in your arm, hand and fingers, it is a particularly valuable tool for contacting your subconscious. Everyday quandaries, such as, 'Can I be bothered to go to the party tonight?' can be put directly to the pendulum. The response – 'yes' or 'no' – will come from your subconscious, which knows exactly how tired you will be, will have a perfectly clear perception of how good the party is likely to be, and will also be aware of 1,001 little details that might have slipped your conscious mind, such as, 'Oh yes, Kate was invited... and she might bring Farouk, and I'd like to meet Farouk again!'

Often, your subconscious can warn you against trusting someone who has conned your conscious mind. 'Should I invite Rav in for a drink next time?' 'Should I put my money into Alexis's business scheme?' 'Should I get a doctor to give me a second opinion?' Remember, the final decision is taken by your conscious mind, so there's no need to worry about falling prey to superstitious mumbo jumbo. In fact, there is more danger of surreptitiously trying to tweak the pendulum thread to give you the response that you hope to see!

It is quite important to quieten your emotions before asking any question of the pendulum that raises strong feelings in you. Experience, perseverance and being honest with yourself will be your best guides in this fascinating voyage of self-exploration.

Using your pendulum on special occasions
A pendulum is commonly used to discern the sex of an unborn child. Whether dowsing directly on the mother-to-be, a photo of her, or even just a strongly imagined thought of her, it is prudent to first ask the pendulum: 'Is this adult female?' Once you are satisfied with that initial response, you can move your attention to the baby itself: 'Is this baby female?'

Although there is a 50:50 chance of getting the sex right by mere chance, it is an important question, and a wrong diagnosis will not be quickly forgotten by the parents. In such delicate circumstances it is well worth taking pains to double-check the answer by asking: 'Is this baby male?'

Obviously, your own subconscious is not in any position to know whether an unborn baby is male or female, so it is a much deeper connection that dowsers are making when they ask questions such as these.

By spreading a map on a table, and slowly moving the pendulum over its whole surface, you can even try to locate missing persons, lost pets, mislaid or even stolen items, buried treasure and valuable mineral deposits, or even healing ley lines, by repeatedly asking: 'Is [name] here?'

Map dowsing is particularly popular, as it is so versatile. It can be used to solicit an answer from a map of the world by asking: 'Should I spend my holiday here?' Or you can use a sketch of the house and garden to ask: 'Is my missing earring here?' or 'Are my lost keys here?'

Furthermore, you can make a series of simple cards, each bearing a single word, such as the names of dates, people, places, jobs or anything else that interests you.

Place the cards in a crescent or horseshoe shape, concentrate on the question, and watch towards which card the pendulum swings: that card reveals the answer. You may prefer to shuffle the cards and have them face down, so that you do not consciously influence the pendulum. And do remember to treat these answers as interesting guidance only, not as destiny written in stone!

A FINAL WISH

Crystals and other stones have long held a fascination for the human race. While science explores the physical attributes of crystals (the first laser, for example, had a ruby at its heart), and is poised for greater discoveries to come, we can all undertake a great adventure into the inner mind and explore the world of the spirit – territory to which science has so far been unable to find a gateway. Many people discover that crystals and other stones can be their passport to a great personal adventure.

It is in this spirit of continuous self-discovery that we leave the future in your hands: hold it safely, for who knows what wonders yet may come to be.

STARS

Wearing crystals as jewellery is a way of bringing them, literally, close to you. If any of the stones for your star sign are not commonly used in jewellery, you can buy a ready-made silver wire spiral and place the crystal inside it. The choice of silver is appropriate as this is the metal of the moon, which boosts your receptiveness to the influence of the stone you're wearing.

If you have body-piercings, try obtaining beads of the appropriate stones with which to close the ends of the body jewellery... having first ensured they are safe to wear!

	RULING STONE	SUN STONE	MOON STONE
ARIES	Ruby	Imperial topaz	White marble
TAURUS	Emerald	Amber	Desert rose
GEMINI	Double terminator rock crystal	Citrine	Apophyllite
CANCER	Moonstone	Aragonite	Silver
LEO	Tiger's eye	Gold	Diamond
VIRGO	Rock crystal egg	Petrified or opalized wood	Stilbite Milky quartz
LIBRA	Chrysoprase	Pyrites	Selenite
SCORPIO	Serpentine	Sulphur Golden beryl	White opal
SAGITTARIUS	Sapphire	Rutilated quartz	White calcite
CAPRICORN	Jet	Yellow jasper	White chalcedony
AQUARIUS	Kunzite	Brown zircon Chiastolite	Optical calcite
PISCES	Black opal	Tiger iron	White aragonite

ARIES		TAURUS	
Weakness, indecision, lack of strength	**Ruby:** wear ruby to promote stamina, forcefulness and determination.	Inflexibility, resistance to change	**Quartz cluster:** Place the cluster somewhere prominent to promote diplomacy and pragmatism. Looking at crystals in a group or cluster, rather than as individual wands, enables you to observe relationships, as if in a family. This is ideal for occasionally autocratic Taureans!
Inability to concentrate, impatience, a tendency to exaggerate	**Rock crystal wand:** Used as a talisman, the rock crystal wand will encourage Arians to project their energy into specific projects rather than squandering it in all directions. It promotes mental alertness, adaptability and the ability to alleviate nightmares and promote sleep.	Emotional dullness, romantic apathy	**Emerald:** Wear emeralds as jewellery or carry them as talismans to aid expression of love and foster harmonious relationships.
Nightmares, insomnia	**Imperial topaz:** Keep this stone close to the bed or under the pillow to alleviate nightmares and promote sound sleep.	Sluggishness	**Desert rose:** Keep this fragile stone close by to enliven mind, body and spirit.
Emotional stress	**White marble:** The protective qualities of this stone will help guard against and relieve emotional trauma.	Obstinacy, stolidness, a tendency to create obstacles	**Garnet** (and any of the red-coloured garnet group of minerals): Garnets have a reputation for exciting interest, dispelling depression, strengthening the heart and improving blood circulation. They are best worn as jewellery to encourage tenacity and guard against inflexibility.
A tendency to be headstrong, incautious and impulsive	**Black flint:** Use this opaque form of chalcedony to promote patience, a sense of duty and caution.	Extravagance, self-indulgence, poor memory	**Azurite nodules:** Although azurite can form transparent, glassy crystals, it also forms granular, dull and opaque nodules that perfectly express the earthy Taurean nature. As a healing stone, it has a reputation for enlivening psychic abilities, especially in divination. It promotes charitable actions, good memory and self-understanding.
Rebelliousness, recklessness	**Purple fluorite:** Handling this stone can impart a sense of natural order and help to structure thoughts. Turning a crystal from facet to facet while going over an idea in your mind can promote lateral thinking and spark new ideas.	Workaholic tendencies	**Galena:** This heavy mineral contains 86 per cent lead and a small amount of silver. Like the Taurean nature, it is very protective. It promotes self-discipline, frugality and management ability. Lead is also toxic, so galena must be handled with care. Anyone wishing to use galena should place it in a glass-fronted cabinet where it can be seen but not accidentally touched.

GEMINI		CANCER	
Impatience, restlessness	**Citrine:** This stone is thought to promote psychic awareness and, when used as a meditation stone, helps to clarify thoughts and ideas.	Overeating	**Moonstone:** Because of its association with the moon and the moon's cycle, moonstone is thought to help regulate eating habits so that they correspond to a more natural ebb and flow, balancing a tendency to overindulge and encouraging a healthier appetite.
Inability to express or tackle intense emotions	**Apophyllite** can help Geminis feel more comfortable about developing their self-understanding, showing those capricious, inconstant people that emotion can be a beautiful thing!	A run of bad luck	**Silver:** Popular as a talisman for attracting good luck and warding off misfortune, silver may be worn as an overall protection against the trials of life.
Fickleness, aloofness	**Moldavite:** This glass-like, non-crystalline mineral has a grounding effect, acting to remind Geminis that, while their ideas and theories may be wonderful, they won't serve much purpose unless put into practice! It also promotes good humour and an affectionate response to friends.	Muddled thoughts, illogicality	**Tumble-polished rock crystal:** The best specimens for Cancer give the impression of a solid droplet of water. They should be used as meditation stones, allowing the mind a clearer insight into its own processes.
Lack of self-assertiveness, a tendency to tire easily	**Fire opal:** This translucent gem can appear to contain red and orange flames when light plays upon it and has a reputation as a passionate stone. It has an enlivening and refining effect, making it appropriate for Geminis who are often lacking in emotional intensity.	Emotional insecurity, 'clinginess'	**Amazonite** (also called amazonstone): This pastel green or blue-green stone is opaque and faintly mottled with lighter hues. When turned in bright light, it radiates a silky, faint sparkle. It is a very 'earthy', worldly stone, representing the Cancerian's considerable strength of character, and is useful for grounding all the emotions.
Superficiality	**Dumorturite:** The whole stone can be faintly sparkling and, used as a meditation or 'worry' stone, shows Geminis that surface gloss isn't everything: sometimes it's necessary to look more deeply to find beauty and value.	Moodiness, frustration, stress-related illnesses	**Rose quartz:** The shell-pink colour of this stone inspires comfort, relaxation and gentle warmth. Modern associations include sweetness, peace, contentment and joy. It is seen as an essentially feminine stone, particularly appropriate for nursing or new mothers, and useful for enhancing the maternal aspects of Cancerians.
Irrationality, confusion	**Stibnite:** Dark silver or grey-hued specimens act to concentrate Gemini's mercurial mind on more rational, practical paths. However, stibnite is toxic, so handle with care. The long, straight crystals encourage Geminis to think logically. They make ideal ornaments which, kept at the workplace, will help focus the mind.	Tension, changeability, fanciful ideas	**Blue fluorite:** Worn as jewellery or used for meditation, blue fluorite can bring out the best of Cancer's considerable interpersonal skills! Fluorite has been used as an ornamental stone since Classical times. It is reputed to quieten emotions and calm thoughts, making it ideal for meditation and highly appropriate for the occasionally overwrought Cancerian.

LEO		VIRGO	
Arrogance, self-importance	**Rainbow aura:** This is a manufactured item created by vaporizing platinum over the natural facets of a clear quartz crystal. This stone may help remind Leos that they are not the only people in existence and to learn to take others into account!	Stress, hyperactivity and anxiety	**Rock crystal egg:** The smooth, comforting shape of the 'worry egg' can help to ease stress and calm down an overactive mind.
Lack of self-confidence	**Gold:** When worn, gold serves as a symbol of the status Leos feel they deserve, and so helps to reassure them of their own worth.	Obstinacy	**Petrified wood:** This aged stone can act as a reminder that too rigid a mental structure can result in a static, stagnant mind, much as a once-living, breathing, growing tree has been changed into stone.
Confusion, bewilderment	**Diamond:** The durability of diamond means it can help clear delirium and cut through muddled thinking, making it perfect for big-hearted but sometimes bewildered Leos!	Ill health	**Milky quartz:** Traditionally, this stone promotes swift recovery and steady recuperation. You can either drink a milky quartz crystal essence remedy (see pages 54–56) or keep the stones within reach so that they may be frequently handled.
Jealousy, vanity	**Malachite:** Talismanically, solid, earthy malachite acts to calm the sometimes overpowering fiery nature of Leo in love.	Frustration, frigidity	**Epidote:** Also called pistacite because of its pistachio green colour, this is a hard, green and cream mottled stone that is particularly comforting to hold and handle. This is an excellent meditation stone and can promote delicacy in intimate relationships.
Inability to concentrate	**Sunstone:** This stone may be placed where the light can catch it to foster a vigorous approach to work. A small mobile hung in the window of the office would be ideal.	Tiredness, irritability, nervousness	**Rhodochrosite:** also known as rosinca or 'Inca rose'. The rose-pink variety of this mineral is perfect here. On the one hand, this stone is thought to increase physical strength and stamina; on the other, it can relax the body and bring a sense of forgiveness and love. Either property is fine for a Virgoan.
Lack of direction	**Smoky quartz:** Traditionally, this stone is used to lift depression, encourage pragmatism and boost enthusiasm. It can help Leos take control of their lives.	A tendency to be obsessive about work	**Basalt:** Although it can be dark grey, the pure black form is best used here. A basalt letter opener, for example, or other useful implement that can be kept in the workplace is most useful here. Touched or handled frequently, it can encourage a sensible attitude to work.

LIBRA		SCORPIO	
Depression, moodiness	**Chrysoprase:** Chrysoprase can focus the mind on the physical aspects of life and promote enjoyment of the simple things. It is a 'feel-good' stone – touching it can promote feelings of happiness and of being at one with the world.	Stress, anxiety	**Serpentine:** Handle serpentine 'worry eggs' – their hard, cool smoothness and comforting weight will help to relieve stress. Meditating on the stone's patterns and colours can also open up the mind to new experiences.
Distraction, a tendency to be unrealistic	**Pyrites:** This stone helps Librans who are prone to being easily distracted from the matter at hand. Its heavy solidity can help bring them back down to earth.	Feeling miserable, pessimistic	**Sulphur:** The sunny colour and unique characteristics of the stone show Scorpios that beauty can be found in the strangest of places! Sulphur should be handled as little as possible, but may be kept on show in a display case, where it can act to bring cheer to its environment.
Indecisiveness, lack of conviction	**Faceted quartz:** There are many shapes of faceted quartz available and all are suitable here, although a square/baguette cut is best. By carefully polishing, the stone is stripped of its irregular faces to create a 'perfect' shape. This makes it ideal for perfection-seeking Librans, helping them to be analytical and persuasive.	Lack of self-control or self-confidence	**White opal:** This is an ideal talismanic stone for Scorpios who are prone to angry outbursts, or who do not value themselves highly enough.
Lack of confidence or courage	**Pink tourmaline:** This transparent stone has a reputation for attracting kind thoughts and is useful in winning affection, trust and prestige. The redder varieties tend also to inspire confidence, bravery and honour.	Prejudice, intolerance	**Rainbow quartz:** Also called iris quartz, this stone can be distinguished from other natural forms of clear quartz by its internal flaws, which refract light in subtle yet spectacular ways. The clarity of the stone can focus the mind and encourage perception, while the lovely internal rainbows can persuade Scorpio to look for beauty, even where there appears to be none.
A tendency to be easily swayed by others' opinions	**Blue agate:** This is a beautiful translucent stone, varying in colour from bright pallid blue to the soft warm blue of early twilight. It is an immensely comforting stone to handle and should help Librans in their struggle for balance.	Jealousy, inner conflict	**Bloodstone:** This opaque stone, also called heliotrope, is a green variety of chalcedony, speckled with red spots of iron oxide which gave rise to its common name. The Egyptians believed it could help free them from shackles, demolish barriers and open doors, allowing them to escape their enemies. This makes it perfect for helping Scorpios, to 'open the door' to their own psyches.
Over-sensitivity to criticism	**Malachite and azurite:** Although azurite is rarer than malachite, they are often found together. Azurite alters to become malachite by reacting with common elements during weathering. Can be used to remind Librans of their own worth and the validity of their own ideas.	Restlessness, an inability to relax	**Red aventurine:** This translucent mineral is usually green, often banded with tiny spots of colour and spangled with glittery mica flakes. Traditionally an all-round healing stone, it can also be used to promote insight, keen perception and help Scorpios in exploring their inner selves. The red variety is associated with relieving headaches, high blood pressure and depression.

SAGITTARIUS		CAPRICORN	
Materialism, boastfulness, dogmatism	**Sapphire:** This precious gem can help balance these typically Sagittarian traits. It is also said to counter both physical and spiritual blindness.	Weakness, irresolution	**Jet:** This stone is best worn as jewellery to promote strength of character and determination in the face of adversity.
Indecision, confusion	**White calcite:** The clarity of this stone may help Sagittarians by acting as a focus for logical thought and decisive action.	Inability to cope with others' demands	**Yellow jasper:** Capricorns are often seen as utterly dependable and so can often feel pressurized when others are leaning on them or making demands on their time. Carrying tumble-polished jasper can help to ease the strain.
Lack of co-ordination or staying power	**Window quartz:** Windows are found near the tips of some quartz wands. Depending on whether the window leans to the left or right, it is said to be either left-handed or right-handed. Right-handed windows are thought to stimulate the emotions and intuition, left-handed windows are associated with the intellect. Occasionally, crystals have both, and these are symbolic of uniting the two sides of the brain and enabling tremendous creative potential – perfect for aspiring Sagittarians.	Seriousness, lack of humour	**White chalcedony:** Capricorns tend to take themselves very seriously. White chalcedony's bright, smooth whiteness encourages them to see the lighter side of life.
Unwillingness to participate in new adventures, fecklessness	**Prehnite:** Prehnite is a superb meditation stone that should keep even Sagittarians' restless minds occupied! Ideally, carry (or wear) a polished stone or keep a natural stone by the bed or on the desk. Wavellite symbolizes the restless nature of Sagittarius, and may be kept as a talisman of journeys taken or new journeys to come.	Self-centredness	**Jade nephrite:** A form of jade, can be white, brown, purple, or most famously, green, which can be mottled with black. Also translucent jadeite is most often found in shades of green, or white with green spots. Both stones may be worn as jewellery, but even a small carved piece can help with issues of constancy, protectiveness and nurturing.
Impulsive behaviour, tactlessness	**Carnelian:** The name is derived from the Latin word, meaning 'flesh' and thus the stone is associated with healing wounds, as well as with stimulating carnal appetites. Sagittarians may wear or handle the stone to give added impetus to their search for wisdom!	Prurience, inconstancy	**Red jasper:** This opaque form of chalcedony is usually bright red due to the presence of iron oxide. Specimens are often veined or marked with dark, even black, streaks. Carry a tumble-polished piece of red jasper and handle it whenever stamina, persistence and strength of will are required!
Difficulty in solving problems or overcoming obstacles	**Obsidian:** There are many varieties of dark obsidian, including 'apache tear', which is particularly well placed here. Talismanically, obsidian is used to help overcome the many and varied obstacles that life throws in our paths at all turns!	Slapdash attitudes, lack of conscience	**Eilat stone:** This is an opaque, blue-green mineral that is a combination of chrysocolla, turquoise and malachite and can be mounted and worn in a ring, so that its energy is ever-present. It promotes professionalism and a clear conscience.

AQUARIUS		PISCES	
Lack of self-discipline	**Kunzite:** This lilac or purple transparent gem can be used to foster self-discipline and a sense of responsibility in Aquarians.	Lack of self-confidence	**Black opal:** This gem encourages Pisceans to explore their own depths and to be true to themselves, rather than try to be what other people expect them to be. Black opals are best worn as jewellery – but take care not to drop them as they are very fragile.
Difficulty in solving problems, unwillingness to compromise	**Optical calcite:** A great meditation stone for helping Aquarians see the middle ground – something they often badly need because often their views are very black and white. Optical calcite can shed light on dilemmas and difficulties.	Having unrealistic goals or dreams	**Tigeriron:** This dark but fascinating stone can act as an anchor for Pisceans, focusing their sparkling minds on the realities of daily life.
Lack of sympathy for others' ideas, aggressive bluntness	**Quartz sphere:** This is the true crystal ball – but beware of glass imitations! A quartz sphere can promote an understanding of obscure ideas, and also objectivity, sensitivity and sympathy for other people's thoughts and views.	Mood swings, feeling over-emotional	**Aragonite:** The solidity of this stone can help counterbalance Piscean's occasional instability of thought and emotion. It is best kept as a small ornament, somewhere prominent but safe in the room in which you spend most time.
Shyness	**Aventurine:** This translucent mineral is regarded as an all-round healing stone. It has the reputation of promoting insight and heightening awareness. It may also bring luck in games of chance, presumably by enhancing precognitive abilities! It is best used as a 'worry' stone or for meditation to boost spontaneity and freedom of expression.	Prejudice, listlessness	**Rock crystal phantom:** This is a rock crystal, usually a wand, within which the image of another crystal can be seen as if growing inside the parent. Fascinating to examine and explore, they make excellent meditation stones. Small stones can be carried and used as a reminder to listen to others and to promote intelligence.
Clinical, cold attitude to others	**Rhodonite:** The cheerful appearance of this stone is held to promote balance, engender a sense of proportion, a sense of humour and humanitarian feelings. Carry a tumble-polished stone and handle it whenever you feel your love for your fellow human-beings waning!	A tendency to be too submissive	**Dioptase:** Once seen in its crystal form, this beautiful rich green stone is hard to forget. Worn as jewellery or kept in a crystal cluster on a desk or bedside table, dioptase promotes tenderness and selfless love, while balancing the Piscean tendency to be overly submissive and conciliatory.
Unreliability	**Iolite:** Also called water sapphire or dichroite, this is a gem-quality variety of cordierite. When viewed from the side, many iolite crystals appear yellow, while from the base they are a deep blue. A great focus for meditation, this crystal promotes co-operation, respect for others and democratic values.	Lack of sexual desire, discontentment	**Dragon's eye:** Here, the golden chatoyancy of the yellow tiger's eye is replaced by a beautiful burgundy. Try keeping a tumble-polished stone, or as large a sphere as you can afford, beside the bed to promote sensuality and playfulness.

INDEX OF CRYSTALS

This edition first published in the United Kingdom in 2022 by
Collins & Brown
43 Great Ormond Street
London
WC1N 3HZ

An imprint of Pavilion Books Company Ltd

Distributed in the United States and Canada by
Sterling Publishing Co., Inc. 1166 Avenue of the Americas, New York, NY 10036

ISBN 978-1-911163-87-9

A CIP catalogue record for this book is available from the British Library.

10 9 8 7 6 5 4 3 2 1

Reproduction by Rival Colour Ltd, UK
Printed and bound by Toppan Leefung Ltd, China

Publisher: Helen Lewis
Editor: Izzy Holton
Designer: Alice Kennedy-Owen
Production Controller: Jessica Arvidsson
Copy Editor: Lucy Bannell
Proofreader: Vicki Murrell
Illustrator: Amy Blackwell

www.pavilionbooks.com